Preface

Hotel industry plays an active role in increasing the employment opportunities and economic status of developed and developing countries and is closely linked to the tourism industry. The success and survival of hotel industry depend upon proper service to customer, cleanliness, acceptable hospitality, proper rooms and other facilities, proper customer-relation management, quality employees, and proper place. However, revenue from hotel and restaurant industry in India during the financial year 2006-07 was Rs.604.32 billion, a growth of 21.27 per cent over the previous year, primarily driven by foreign tourist arrivals that increased by 14.17 per cent. The hospitality industry is expected to grow at a faster rate and reach Rs.826.76 billion by 2010.

The hotel industry constitutes a very important sector of the touristic infrastructure and is considered the king-pin of the tourist industry. It has been aptly said "No Hotels, No Tourism". Among the numerous types of facilities, sought by the tourists, transport and accommodation form the important items. In this study, "accommodation" is assumed to be the first and the foremost infrastructure, necessary to improve tourist traffic. It is rightly said that "the accommodation facilities are the places where tourists stop (cease to be travellers) and become guests. The level of guest satisfaction achieved by an area's accommodation facilities will, in a large measure, determine the total success of the tourism programme.

Tourism has emerged as the most lucrative business of the world, having tremendous potential for earning foreign exchange. Globally speaking, tourism accounts for nearly 5.4 per cent of world's trade and 11 per cent of world's gross product. In the global market of 400 million tourists, India's share constitutes, at present, a meagre 0.35 per cent. In modern times, tourism has received the widest recognition and it is the second largest industry in the world while it is the sixth largest in India.

Tourism in India has a vast employment potential much, of which still awaits exploitation. Another important aspect of employment in tourism is that it employs a large number of women in hotels, airlines services, travel agencies, handicrafts business and marketing and cultural activity centres. In other words, every man, woman and child could become richer by Rs.7,000. India has yet to realize its full potentials in tourism. The travel and tourism industry holds tremendous potential for India's economy. It can provide impetus to other industries, create millions of new jobs and generate enough wealth to help pay off international debt. That is why we have included tourism amongst the core sectors of the Indian economy.

This book has covered all the major segments of the subject and is divided into seven chapters spread over the following topics – Introduction and design of the study, The tourists attractions in Kanyakumari District, The hotel industry scenario, The trends in tourist arrivals and hotel accommodation in Kanyakumari, The profile of the tourists, expenditure portfolio and its determinants, An- analysis of the hotel industry in Kanyakumari, The summary of the findings of the analysis, conclusion arrived at and offers suitable policy implications. I hope it would serve as a useful text and reference book for all categories of readers, particularly academics, researchers, practitioners and government agencies.

Any constructive criticism and suggestion is always welcome.

Dr. R. Ahila

Dr. X. Antony Thanaraj

ROLE OF HOTEL INDUSTRY IN THE PROMOTION OF TOURISM

By

Dr. R. Ahila

M.Com.M.Phil, Ph.D.
Lecturer
Hindustan College of Arts and Science, Chennai
Madras University, Tamil Nadu
(India)

&

Dr. X. Antony Thanaraj

Associate Professor
Dept. of Commerce
Scott Christian College, Nagercoil
Manonmaniam Sundaranar University
(Tamil Nadu)
(India)

DISCOVERY PUBLISHING HOUSE PVT. LTD.
NEW DELHI-110 002

Published by:
Tilak Wasan
DISCOVERY PUBLISHING HOUSE PVT. LTD.
4383/4B, Ansari Road, Darya Ganj
New Delhi-110 002 (India)
Phone : +91-11-23279245, 43596064-65
Fax : +91-11-23253475
E-mail : discoverypublishinghouse@gmail.com
sales@discoverypublishinggroup.com
parul.wasan@gmail.com
web : www.discoverypublishinggroup.com

First Edition: **2013**

ISBN: 978-93-5056-295-6

Role of Hotel Industry in the Promotion of Tourism

Printed at:
Dynamic Printers
Delhi

Contents

availed—The most delightful tourism activity in Kanyakumari —Arrangement of the tour—Distribution of tourists on the purpose of their visit to Kanyakumari—Hotel Accommodation and Expenditure Portfolio of Selected Tourists—Sources of information about the hotel—Mode of transport used to reach the hotel—Average number of days in India stayed by foreign tourists—Actual stay as against the original plan—Tourists' preference as to the category of hotels—Reasons for selection of one to three star hotels by foreign tourists—Tourists' preference to the plan types—Types of rooms preferred by the Tourists—Tourists Evaluation of Hotel Facilities and Services—Factors influencing the choice of hotels —Method of booking hotel rooms by the tourists—Tourists' general preference to the location of hotels—Location of hotels preferred by domestic tourists —Location of hotel stayed in by foreign tourists—Domestic tourists' opinion about the area of hotels—Foreign tourists opinion about the area of hotels —Food habits—Domestic tourists' opinion about the prices charged—Foreign tourists' opinion about the prices charged—Domestic tourists' opinions on the taste of food and beverage—Foreign tourists' opinion about the taste of food and beverage —Domestic tourists' opinion about décor, furnishing and furniture in hotels at Kanyakumari—Foreign tourists' opinion about décor, furnishing and furniture in the hotels in Kanyakumari—Domestic tourists' opinion about the various services and facilities in star category hotels—Foreign tourists' opinion about the various services and facilities in star category hotels—Average hotel expenses by the domestic and foreign tourists—Opinion of the foreign tourists

List of Abbreviations

A/C	Air Conditioning
AD	Anno Domini
ANOVA	Analysis of variance
CTV	Cable Television
CIS	Commonwealth of Independent States
FHRAI	Federation of Hotel & Restaurant Association of India
GDP	Gross Domestic Product
HCI	Hotel Corporation of India
IIT	Indian Institute of Tourism
IITTM	Indian Institute of Tourism and Travel Management
IMF	International Monetary fund
INR	Indian Rupee
ITC	International Trade Commission
ITDC	Indian Tourism Development Corporation
ITHI	Indian Tourism and Hotel Industry
IT	Information Technology
MGF	Mobile Giving Foundation
MHPU	Ministry of Housing and Public Utilities
MICE	Meetings, Incentives, Conventions and Exhibitions
MNC	Multi National Corporation
MT	Ministry of Tourism
NCHMCT	National Council for Hotel Management and Catering Technology

SAARC	South Asia Association of Regional Corporation
SEA	South East Asian
TTDC	Tamil Nadu Tourism Development Corporation
UNWTO	United Nations World Trade Organisation
US	United States
USD	United States Dollars
WTTC	World Travel and Tourism Council

CHAPTER 1

Introduction and Design of The Study

Introduction

Hotel industry plays an active role in increasing the employment opportunities and economic status of developed and developing countries and is closely linked to the tourism industry. The success and survival of hotel industry depend upon proper service to customer, cleanliness, acceptable hospitality, proper rooms and other facilities, proper customer-relation management, quality employees, and proper place. However, revenue from hotel and restaurant industry in India during the financial year 2006-07 was Rs.604.32 billion, a growth of 21.27 per cent over the previous year, primarily driven by foreign tourist arrivals that increased by 14.17 per cent. Currently, there are 1,934 hotels approved and classified by the Ministry of Tourism, Government of India, with a total capacity of about 1,03,973 hotel rooms. The hospitality industry is expected to grow at a faster rate and reach Rs.826.76 billion by 2010. It is estimated that over the next two years 70,000-80,000 rooms will be added across different categories throughout the country. With this backdrop this study has been undertaken to analyse the satisfaction level of customers on the services of hotel industry. According to Philip Kotler (2006) customer satisfaction refers to the individual feelings of pleasure or disappointment resulting from comparing a profit - perceived performance in relation to his or her expectation. Westbrook & Oliver (1991) feel that customer satisfaction is a post consumption evaluative judgment, concerning a specific product or service. However, customer satisfaction is a measure of how products or services supplied by an industry meets customer expectation and it is an ambigious and abstract concept and the actual manifestation of the state of satisfaction will vary from person to person. The performance of an organisation is purely based on consumer satisfaction. If the organisation does not take proper steps towards satisfaction consumers, it may adversely impact on the profitability of the organisation.[1]

The hotel industry constitutes a very important sector of the touristic infrastructure and is considered the king-pin of the tourist industry. It has been aptly said "No Hotels, No Tourism". Among the numerous types of facilities, sought by the tourists, transport and accommodation form the important items. In this study, "accommodation" is assumed to be the first and the foremost infrastructure, necessary to improve tourist traffic. It is rightly said that "the accommodation facilities are the places where tourists stop (cease to be travellers) and become guests. The level of guest satisfaction achieved by an area's accommodation facilities will, in a large measure, determine the total success of the tourism programme.[2]

Tourism has emerged as the most lucrative business of the world, having tremendous potential for earning foreign exchange. Globally speaking, tourism accounts for nearly 5.4 per cent of world's trade and 11 per cent of world's gross product. In the global market of 400 million tourists, India's share constitutes, at present, a meagre 0.35 per cent.[3] In modern times, tourism has received the widest recognition and it is the second largest industry in the world while it is the sixth largest in India.

India has much to offer, both to the foreign and domestic tourists. In fact, it is no exaggeration to say that no other single tourist destination in the world has a greater and diverse range of tourist attractions than India.[4]

India's tourist attractions are many. Its historic and cultural mosaic is, indeed, unique. Indian civilization is a combination of Vedic, Islamic and Western streams. Its monuments, sculptures and paintings, bear testimony to the national ethos for harmony and diversities. Its geographical features are both colourful and varied. India has the lofty Himalayas, to inspire human spirit to divine heights. It has some of the best beaches of the world, with an irresistible combination of Sun, Sand and Sea. It has a chain of bird sanctuaries and national parks. It also has some of the best hill-resorts. In addition to all these fairs and festivals are in abundance. In spite of such attractions, India's share constitutes less than half-a-per cent, mainly, because of insufficient infrastructure. However, it is heartening to know that the earnings in terms of foreign exchange from tourism are generally on the increase, in India. To be more specific, its earnings were just 31.5 crores of rupees in 1971 and it increased and touched the level of Rs.1,063 crores of rupees in 1981.[5]

The earnings from tourism rose to Rs.2,440 crores in 1991 and it is expected that by the end of the present century, the amount will increase to Rs.10,000 crores.[6]

Several agencies in India, are involved to develop and promote tourism at national and international level. The agencies are (1) Department of Tourism; (2) Indian Institute of Tourism; (3) India Tourism Development; (4) Travel Management; and (5) National Council for Hotel Management and Catering Technology.

The Department of Tourism is responsible for the promotion of India as a tourist destination, development of tourism infrastructure and facilities in the country. It also performs regulatory functions in the field of tourism. There are four regional offices in Delhi, Bombay, Calcutta and Madras.

The Indian Institute of Tourism and Travel Management

was set up in January 1983, with its registered office at New Delhi. It is designed as an institute for offering different level academic courses in the field of tourism and travel management and related areas.

India Tourism Development Corporation, a public sector undertaking, established in October 1966, is responsible for creation, development and expansion of tourism. It provides varied services to tourists, by way of accommodation, catering, transport, entertainment, shopping facilities, conventions, etc. It also produces, distributes and sells tourist publicity material and renders consultancy services in the field of tourism, both in India and abroad.

The National Council for Hotel Management and Catering Technology, with its headquarters in New Delhi, acts as an apex body to co-ordinate training and research in hotel and catering management.[7]

Contribution of Tourism Industry to Indian Economy

Tourism is one of the fastest growing sectors in the country. It offers immense opportunities to entrepreneurs in various segments. But what is detrimental to our tourism growth is lack of basic facilities at our monuments, pilgrimage places and tourist sites. We need to improve the basic facilities by roping in all the stakeholders, as the government cannot do this job alone. The Asia region is as important for us as other regions and we are going to aggressively market there.

Tourism industry is largely attributed to a rise in global wealth, liberalization of international airspace, cheaper flights and the use of the internet as a travel tool. Interestingly, a recent study has found that India, today, ranks eighth in the world, in terms of the number of billionaires and has over 1.6 million households that earn over Rs.45 lakhs per year and spend about Rs.4 lakhs, on luxury on premium goods and services. So, it is estimated that Indian tourism market potential is worth Rs.65,000 crores and the number of such households is growing at the rate of 14 per cent.[8]

Another healthy trend in foreign tourism in India since 1991 is the conspicuous increase in business travels with its spinoff effects in the upgradation of accommodation and introduction of new technology in communications and other services. On an average, a foreign tourist stays for about 27 days in India which is an important indicator of increase of the foreign exchange, earned by the country.

Recent political unrest, fear of violence, terrorism, strikes, epidemics etc., are detrimental to our tourism business. However, considering the recent developments, it is hoped that India will get her share in world tourism. Marketing of tourism services, includes mainly the services sold to domestic and foreign tourists. Domestic tourism fosters a sense of unity is otherwise diverse environment of the country and contributes to national integration.

Tourism in India has a vast employment potential much, of which still awaits exploitation. Another important aspect of employment in tourism is that it employs a large number of women in hotels, airlines services, travel agencies, handicrafts business and marketing and cultural activity centres. In other words, every man, woman and child could become richer by Rs.7,000. India has yet to realize its full potentials in tourism. The travel and tourism industry holds tremendous potential for India's economy. It can provide impetus to other industries, create millions of new jobs and generate enough wealth to help pay off international debt. That is why we have included tourism amongst the core sectors of the Indian economy.[9]

Hotel sector is the key segment of tourism industry to earn foreign exchange. Places of tourist interest are so numerous and of varied nature that it is not easy to describe these places comprehensively. These include mostly, the Himalayan region, the Great Plain of north India, the Peninsular Plateau and coastal plains. In general, the tourist spots are counted more like Buddhist sites, shrines, forts, places of historical importance, hot springs, Jain monasteries, lakes and bird sanctuaries, religious centres, science spots, sea beaches, summer resorts, waterfalls and wild life sanctuaries.

Tourism involves travelling to relatively undisturbed or uncontaminated natural areas, with the specific objects of studying, admiring and enjoying the scenery and the wild flora and fauna, as well as other existing cultural and historical aspects. A visit with a desire to know these areas is nothing but tourism. Places of tourist interest are numerous and of varied nature. These include places of archeological and historical importance, pilgrimage centres, sanctuaries, national parks, hill resorts and sea beaches.

In order to give a fillip to the tourism trade, the Central Government as well as the State Government, should come forward to develop some of the newly unexploited and selected tourist places, diversify some of the culture oriented tourism to holiday and leisure tourism, develop trekking, winter sports, wild life, beach resort tourism, launching key markets near tourist centres, provide inexpensive accommodation and to improve service efficiency. India hopes still to improve tourism marketing services and to take equal and more challenging steps with her competitors in the field more vigorously.

There is no dearth of tourist destinations in the world. Tourist generating countries are themselves gifted with diverse natural and man- made tourist attractions and therefore they are excellent tourist destinations. So to win targets and attract maximum inbound tourists, creative plans and innovative strategies have to be adopted. A tourist organisation should employ a core group of professionals who will engage in shaping plans, strategies and programmes for implementation. The progress of these actions must be evaluated periodically and if necessary, corrective revision and updating must also be undertaken.

Tourism plays an important role in promoting international goodwill. It creates awareness and appreciation of other countries' culture and tradition and makes possible, cultural exchange and enrichment. In Indian context, the age old saying "Atithi Devo Bhavo" is apt and appropriate. Tourism can be a vehicle for international understanding, by way of bringing diverse people from different cultures and traditions and can greatly enrich and promote friendship between different countries in the world. The socio-economic benefits from tourism are powerful.

Tourism development must be guided by a sound and careful planned policy, a policy not built on balance sheets and profit and loss statements alone, but on the ideals and principles of human welfare and happiness. Sound development policy can have the happy results of a growing tourist business and the preservation of the natural and cultural resources that attracted visitors in the first place. Main advantages of tourism are that it provides employment opportunities, both skilled and unskilled, because it is a labour intensive industry, generates a supply of foreign exchange, increases income, creates increased gross national product, requires the development of an infrastructure that will also help stimulate local commerce and industry, justifies environmental protection and improvement, increases governmental revenues, helps to diversify the economy, creates a favourable worldwide image for the destination, facilitates the process of modernization, by education of youth and society and changing values, provides tourist recreational facilities that may be used by a local population, gives foreigners an opportunity to be favourably impressed by a little known country or region.

Global tourism continued to move upward during 2006, with the number of international tourist arrivals worldwide reaching about 846 million (UNWTO estimates) and international tourism receipts scaling US $ 735 billions in the year. The aforesaid variables grew at 5.7 per cent and 8.4 per cent respectively, compared to 2005. The rate of growth of the tourism sector of India has been above the world average in the last few years, 2006-2007 is the fourth consecutive year of high growth in foreign tourist arrivals and foreign exchange earnings from tourism. Both inbound and outbound tourism from India registered 15 per cent to 20 per cent growth in 2006-07 and is expected to cross 20 per cent this year too. By

2020 tourism in India could contribute Rs.8,50,000 crore to the GDP.

The prospects for growth of tourism in India are bright. The overall development of tourism infrastructure, coupled with other efforts by the government to promote tourism, such as appropriately positioning India in the global tourism map through the "Incredible India" campaign, focusing more on newly emerging markets such as China, Latin America and CIS countries, and participating in trade fairs and exhibitions will facilitate tourism growth.

Year 2007 saw over 5 million foreigners visiting India, generating about $ 12 billion in foreign forex earnings. The bullish trend continues in 2008, with about 12 per cent growth in foreign traffic and 29 per cent of growth in forex earnings in the first four months of the year. The opening of a tourism office in Beijing in April 2008, has opened a new gateway. But India has miles to go before it catches up with its neighbour China, which boasts of 50 million foreign visitors. The success of 'Incredible India' campaign has proved that the potential of the country is immense. On top of an excellent marketing campaign, efforts are being made to create better tourism infrastructure to sustain the growth momentum, at national level by maximizing tourism. 'Incredible India' campaign has been able to capture the high-end tourists, who are spending a longer time in India. This is evident from the UNWTO's latest report which indicates that even though countries like Indonesia, Thailand and Singapore may be having larger number of foreign tourist arrivals, the foreign exchange earned per foreign tourist, by India is much higher (at about $ 1,920) compared to that of Indonesia ($ 905) and Malaysia ($ 520). These facts confirm that India is attracting travellers from across the globe, that are spending more time and money, compared to those from other SEA countries.

In 2007, India received 5 million foreign tourists and had a Foreign Exchange Earning (FEE) of $ 12 billion. Thailand earned a little more than India, about 14 million tourists during the year. While India has been a long-haul tourist destination

Thailand and Malaysia are short haul destination. India is also trying to attract tourists for short – haul destinations. Some important heritage sites are Hampi, Ajanta and Ellora, Bodh Gaya and Taj Mahal. India would also convert more sites into short-haul tourist destinations. For 2008-09, India has a budget of about Rs.1,000 crores to develop tourism infrastructure.

The tourism sector is an economic driver. It directly and indirectly employs about 8.9 per cent of the total work force in the country. Globally, 8.1 per cent people are employed in this sector. We expect a total tourist arrival of 10 millions in 2010 which will lead to huge employment. We are promoting rural tourism, food, medical, tribal, shopping and tea garden, among many other types of tourism. We are also encouraging adventure and sports tourism like rafting and mountain climbing. We expect to have a significant share in the MICE market.

Market Potential of Indian Tourism Industry in Global Perspective

India has a significant potential for becoming a major global tourist destination. The growth in India's tourism market is expected to serve as a boon, stimulating the growth of several associated industries, including hotel industry, medical tourism industry and aviation industry. The following achievements and contributions are enough to prove India's tourism potential in global world:

1. **Travel and tourism:** Travel and tourism is the second highest foreign exchange earner of India, and the government has given organizations in this industry 'export house status'.
2. **Domestic trips:** The industry is waking up to the potential of domestic tourism as well, with 382.1 million domestic trips in 2005 as against 236.5 million domestic trips in 2001.
3. **Exports:** Export earnings from international visitors and tourism goods are expected to generate 6.7 per

cent of total exports of 718.2 billions (INR) or US $ 18.5 billion in 2008, growing (nominal terms) to INR 2,750.2 billion or US $ 51.6 billion (4.4 per cent of the total) in 2018.

4. **Employment:** There is considerable government presence in travel and tourism industry. Each state has a tourism corporation, which typically runs a chain of hotels / motels and operates package tours, while the Central government runs the India Tourism Development Corporation. Divestment of these state-run tourism corporations has either already taken place or is in process. The contribution of the travel and tourism economy to employment, is expected to rise from 30,491,000 jobs in 2008 i.e., 6.4 per cent of total employment or 1 in every 15.6 jobs to 39,615,000 jobs i.e., 7.2 per cent of total employment or 1 in every 13.8 jobs by 2018.
5. **Gross Domestic Product** : The contribution of travel and tourism to Gross Domestic Product is expected to stay the same at 6.1 per cent (INR 2,859 billion or US $ 73.6 billion) in 2008 to 6.1 per cent (INR 9,141.1 billion or US $ 171.5 billion) by 2018.
6. **Growth:** Incoming foreign tourist arrivals have shown a 6 per cent compound annual growth rate over the last 10 years. The government has realized the potential and has advanced several incentives to promote infrastructure growth in the tourism sector. Real GDP growth for travel and tourism economy is expected to be 7.9 per cent in 2008 and to an average 7.6 per cent per annum over the coming 10 years.

Current investments are likely to see hotel room capacity increase, by 20 per cent over the next three years, with several international hotel chains entering the hotel industry. Similar growth is anticipated in air travel capacity also.[10]

Laws Governing the Hotel Industry and Tourism

The laws governing the professional status of the hotel industry, should be subjected to review and amendment, by both governmental authorities and trade organisations. The aim is to provide a suitable environment for hotels and other tourist establishments, so that they may practice their trade under favourable conditions. Emphasis should be placed upon raising the standards, in general. This should cover a broad range of facilities, like furnishings and equipment and also quality of service. It is most important, that the legislation must set up incentives for capital investment.

The laws should deal with regulating the relationship between hotel guests on one hand and the hotel management on the other. It should provide stipulations, regarding rates and the means of controlling them, the procedures for sanctions, including closing and granting of licenses. Standards should also be established for grading hotels and other tourist accommodations in accordance with international practices.

The law may consist of several sections dealing with the following aspects:

Tourist Establishment

These include public establishments that may be authorised by the Ministry of Tourism for accommodating tourists. These are:

(*a*) Hotels
(*b*) Floating Hotels
(*c*) Motels
(*d*) Tourist Shops
(*e*) Tourist Bungalows
(*f*) Rest Houses
(*g*) Tourist Rest Houses
(*h*) Apartments (permitted)
(*i*) Tourist Villages
(*j*) Homes
(*k*) Guest Houses.

The public places that could be licensed by the Ministry of Tourism to offer food and beverages to the tourists are restaurants, bars, night clubs and casinos.

Also included under the Law for Licensing are transport facilities on land, sea and the river water.

For the setting up and management of these establishments, a license must be obtained from the Ministry of Tourism, in accordance with the regulations and procedures defined by the Ministry.

The engineering and structural conditions of such tourist establishments should be specified by the Ministry of Housing and Public Utilities, except floating hotels and transit ships, which are the concern of the Ministry of Transport. In all cases, the Ministry of Tourism should approve such specifications.

Only gambling casinos should be open to non-Indians under the jurisdiction of the Ministry of Tourism, which specifies the places of gambling and the conditions imposed. All dealings in gambling must be in foreign currency.

Taxes

Tourist establishments, including hotels and authorised places defined above, may be exempt from taxes, including taxes on commercial and industrial profits and real estate taxes. These exemptions may be granted for the first five years of operation, beginning with the date when such taxes become due. Income taxes are borne by individuals and are based on the net income of the person.

All capital goods, including building material and equipment, whether for initial erection or for rehabilitation and renovation, are custom-free for authorized tourist establishments.

Operating Personnel

The conditions and standards to be met by hotel personnel are to be defined by the Ministry of Tourism.

Guest Relations

The Act should regulate the relationship between clients and hotels in such matters as refusing to rent out rooms and renting rooms at higher rates than authorised.

Hotel Rates

The determination of tariffs for various services and the grading of tourist establishments are to be covered under this head.

Relation with Ministry of Tourism

The obligations of the tourist establishments need to be spelled out in this section. It includes:

1. Publishing the hotel grade and price of services in both English and Hindi in guest rooms as well as in the reception office.
2. Notify the Ministry monthly, of the number of guest-nights realised.
3. Maintain a reservation register for all requests for room reservations.

These should be made mandatory by the Ministry of Tourism.[11]

Statement of the Problem

Modern tourism is the most striking phenomenon of the 21st Century and offers us an opportunity to learn, enrich humanity and to identify what may be termed as goals, for a better life and a better society. As an industry the impact of tourism is manifold. Tourism industry, nourishes a country's economy, stimulates development process, restores cultural heritage, and helps in maintaining international peace and understanding. The most significant feature of the tourism industry is the capacity to generate large scale employment opportunities. It also contributes to national integration. Tourism consists of diverse operations, ranging from tour operators, travel agencies, hotels, destination development and promotion of airlines, road, rail and water transportation, entertainment, cuisine and so on. In order to develop and promote responsible tourism, one also has to do away with or minimize the negative impacts of tourism, particularly on ecology and environment, culture, customs and traditions of the host population. People, in general, now view tourism as a way of life rather than a luxury item reserved for the affluent and the elite. The tourist has become more cautious of the value of the money he/she spends. This means for the service providers, constant improvement in the quality of the service, maintaining certain standards and greater emphasis on customer care.[12]

Hotel and its management, once regarded as a part, is at present being considered as a science and has therefore been realised that hotels provide an excellent setting for research studies. The problems found in socio-economic and managerial fields, facilitate enormous scope for research by sociologists, economists and psychologists. For example, problems connected with marketing of accommodation, advertising, sales promotion, training, production, communication, recruitment grievances, etc., are all becoming sensitive to the growth and development of hotel industry. Hence, the hotel industry, and particularly, the accommodation sector, is increasingly conscious of the research needs in its various operations. But until recently, no other industry has ever received less attention than hotel and tourism industry in the field of research and this fact is true, particularly in the case of India.

The researcher being fully aware of the need and importance of study about hotel industry, at micro-level in relation to tourist inflow, has undertaken to do so choosing Kanyakumari – a beautiful summer resort in Tamil Nadu as the study area. It is optimistically believed that this modest attempt in this field, will certainly prove to provide some substantial information, in order to frame an adequate policy to tackle the problems connected with hotel industry in Kanyakumari in particular and hotel industry in other parts of tourist interest in India at large.

Review of Literature

During the last decade, a number of studies have been undertaken on various aspects of tourism in India. The investigator makes an attempt to review the most outstanding among them.

Pangi,[13] who has made an in-depth study on the uses of tourism, points out how during the last two decades, tourism has emerged as the world's largest and fastest growing industry. He argues that the importance of tourism rests more on its contribution to the national income. It is known as the multiplier effect associated with the turn over of tourist expenditure. He emphatically adds that every unit of money spent on tourism, circulates in the economy and creates greater and greater benefits to the general public. The economic study conducted by him, on this, aspect has led him to conclude that each tourist rupee spent in India, tends to create a transaction worth Rs. 3.5. In addition to this, the tourism industry, according to Pangi, plays a vital role in the development of tourist spots and creation of infrastructure and marketing facilities.

The factors determining domestic tourism have been dealt with at length by Kunal Chellopedhyay.[14] According to him, domestic tourism develops and assures a significant proportion of total tourist trade as long as two conditions prevail. They are, a large number of tourism-minded people and availability of well-connected tourist sites. Kunal holds, that these two factors are present in an abundant measure in India. However, what is unique about the Indian tourists is that Indians travel thousands of miles on pilgrimages, in spite of their very low-earning potentials.

Francesco Frangialli[15] puts forward five challenges for international tourism up to the turn of the century. They are, to benefit from socio-demographic factors favourable to international tourism and to incorporate technological changes that foster development in order to take advantage of the current tends in consumer behaviour, to opt for a strategy of sustainable development and to develop and improve human resources.

Vivek Sharma[16] has made a study on the socio-economic importance of tourism. Notably, tourism has come to be accepted as a catalyst to economic development and as a potent tool for social integration and foreign exchange earner. The author stresses, that economic importance of tourism can be studied in relation to its contribution to increase in income, foreign exchange earnings, employment, return on investment and conservation of resources.

The tourist traffic gives a boost to production of handicrafts and products of small and village industries and has its spin-off effects on all village industries. These ideas have been upheld also by Shiva Shankar Bhat.[17]

The uses of tourism have been dealt with, in very great detail by Roy.[18] In his opinion, tourism is endowed with the potentials to generate employment opportunities to the literates and the illiterates, the skilled and the unskilled population of a country. Further, it can rejuvenate certain dying cottage and handicrafts industries as well. In fact, it is a complex industry which is closely interrelated with every other sector of the economy.

According to Sharma[19] on tourism, tourism industry will have its spin-off effects on the all-round economic and social development of a country only if environmental changes like better transportation facilities and communication system are brought about with systematic care. In the absence of such environmental changes, the tourism industry would always remain under-developed.

According to Shiv Shankar Bhat's[20] tourism is a major foreign exchange earner and hence the industry should be treated on par with export oriented industries and the same benefits be extended to it. The outlook for tourism is bright if the Central and State Governments decide to step in and help this industry to grow by leaps and bounds. Bhat thinks of some ways to promote tourism in India. It is necessary to create a new environment. Also a new package of infrastructure facilities should be devised.

The evaluation of Joseph[21] about the potential of the tourist market of Kerala suggests measures for the expansion of the same. In summer, tourist potential of Kerala emerge resourceful but is, yet to be fully exploited. Sound policies have to be evolved and implemented if resources are to be tapped to the fullest extent possible. Provision of cheap but neat accommodation and facilities for entertainment would be some of the measures to be taken as a starting point to cater to the needs of tourists.

Tourist attraction has been the main focus of those who specialise in the economics of tourism industry. Joseph[22] who has evinced a very great interest in this area of research, has focused on fourteen major attractions. They include beach resorts, backwaters, scenic beauty, historical monuments, cultural performances, handicrafts, wildlife sanctuaries, mountain resorts, natural vegetation, waterfalls, beaches, temples, sanctuaries and others.

Singh[23] comments on the problems and prospects of tourism marketing in India. The author explains the problems of tourism in the following series of questions:

Why is it that we do not have a fair share in the overall tourist spectrum?

Why is it that only one out of every 250 tourists worldwide wants to visit India despite her enormous tourist potential?

Is there something fundamentally wrong with our tourism development programme?

Also, the author makes some suggestions of special significance in this context. Considering India's vast potential in tourism industry, the government should accord to tourist sector, a high priority. Second factor that deserves attention is developing our beach resorts, hill resorts and resorts at other way-out places, to encourage a balanced development of all regions.

Due stress must be exerted on the development of infrastructural facilities for promoting tourism in the country. For this, we require a substantial injection of funds which may be obtained through local borrowings at concessional rates of interest, from financial institutions. Apart from undertaking vigorous and effective publicity campaigns, efforts must be made to ensure a favourable impression given to all the tourists, landing at our airports and make them feel more at home.

The profile of International Tourism in India has been traced by Kumar B. Dass and Mohanty[24] According to them tourism is the second largest industry of the world and sixth largest in India. The historic and cultural mosaic it presents to foreign tourists is indeed unique. There is an abundance of fairs and festivals in India. 'Product India' boasts of being exceptional and unique in many ways.

The tourism industry is noted for its tremendous social impact. According to Selvam[25] promotion of national integration is possible through tourism development. 'Unity in diversity' could be easily promoted through tourism. As tourists, people forget their own creed, caste, community and religion and increasingly tend to mix with all. Standard of living improves with the development of tourism. Foreign tourism brings precious foreign exchange into the nation. Domestic tourism also results in income transfer. There is a faster rate of growth of employment generation. Tourism promotes many wage-goods industries and the lower strata of people get additional income.

Development of people's knowledge about a region is a social benefit. International understanding is promoted through tourism. Exchange of cultural values and protection of flora and fauna constitute a few other social benefits of tourism. Tourism involves grooming of the youth, harnessing their talents and channelling their energy in the right direction. Youth tourism, sport tourism and adventure tourism will encourage the youth to corne closer and contribute to the common good. Ecological degradation results from unplanned tourism. Tourism is considered as a smokeless industry. But, of late, smoke has begun to surface over and above the flora and fauna of the land, which is increasingly exposed to tourist population. Similarly, there seems to be the over exploitation of community resources like water and power for the exclusive use of tourists.

Ritu Galati[26] observes the prospects and problems of tourism in Uttaranchal. The hilly terrain of Uttar Pradesh konwn as Uttaranachal comprises of eight districts. The author explains that, the U.P. government has announced some special packages for promoting tourism in this area.

Encouragement to hotel industry, Loan Grant Scheme, Luxury Tax, Registration of excursion agencies, the Kailash Mansarovar Yatra and also Tourism Development of Puri and Sheetlakhat are some of them. According to the decision taken by the government, special measures are being taken to develop Puri and Sheetlakhat as new tourist cities.

Veera Sekaran[27] advocates development through tourism sector. According to him, tourism has become a major global activity. Countries like Philippines, Hong Kong, Singapore, Malaysia, etc., have considerably enhanced their economic development through tourism. Hence, tourism has emerged as a special type of development planning.

As a result, tourism has given rise to a special branch of knowledge in economics which will generate direct and indirect employment opportunities.

Thus tourism is an important medium of social and cultural development. It builds lasting goodwill and friendship among different nations. Tourism also helps in regional development of the country and acts as a measure of social education and better understanding, according to Padmanabha Rao.[28]

Ameen A.M. Al-Momani[29] points out the economic gains of tourism industry. The economic gains of tourism include the direct as well as direct effects of expenditure on tourism. Tourism generates foreign exchange for the host countries and it has emerged as the largest single item in the world's foreign trade. Tourism provides employment on a large scale. The ratio of employment capital in this industry is amazingly.

Moreover, provision of infrastructure-communication systems, shops, hospitals, civic amenities etc made for tourists also benefit the local population and their living conditions continue to improve substnatially.

Concerning the beneficiaries of tourism sector, Sarngadharan[30] gives an account of the various categories of beneficiaries in the Indian economy through the systematic development of tourism, which include travel agents, airlines, banks, hotels, transporters, guides, artists, artisans and manufacturers.

The new strategy for Indian tourism industry was pointed out by Vijayakumar.[31] According to him; it should evolve an integrated strategy for the promotion of tourism in a big way. This need assumes considerable importance with a proper emphasis on a comprehensive, long-term approach, in order to achieve sustainable development in harmony with the country's overall development objectives.

Tourism industry needs promotion, according to Navin Chandra Joshi. He calls for widening the areas of interest, creation of more tourist destinations and improvement of infrastructural facilities. He welcomes the move to allow foreign airlines to add to their fleet of passenger-cum-cargo combination.

Tourism, in any nation, is inextricably connected with its environment. According to Sharma,[32] unplanned tourism will always hold the environment of a nation in total jeopardy. In other words, tourism sans planning, will ruin the entire environment. Hence, as Sharma has put it, tourism industry must respond to the aspirations of the environmentalists in a positive way.

Vijaya Kumar T. and Bhagavan[33] while adding to what Sharma has pointed out regarding tourists contributions to environmental degradation, are of the view that tourists are totally responsible for the growth of ruined flowerbeds, polluted lakes, accumulation of garbage in tourist centers, defection in tourist spots and actively contribute to bag nuisance. The ailing culture and negative habits are so infectious that they can easily vitiate the social environment of those who live not far from the 'madding crowds' ignorable strife.[34] Herbmankham, the well-known futurologist, has treated tourism next only to atomic power as far as its potentials for environmental destruction is concerned. Taking these strands of thoughts still further, Shrutidhar Paliwal[35] stresses the need for eco-friendly tourists who can protect not only environment but also contribute sizably to the material growth of a nation. The eco-friendly trips promote a keen sense of good will between the tour participants and the people whom they come into contact with. Thus, according to Paliwal, eco-friendly tourism can add to one's personal awareness about the world and the people.

John[36] while supplementing this view, points out how environmental factors like fresh air, natural landscapes and flora and fauna, attractive beaches, perennial rivers and water falls play a vital role in the growth of tourists. This idea has been upheld by Singa[37]

The hotel industry forms an integral part of the tourism industry in any country. According to Dharmarajan et al.,[38] hotels in India yield more than 300 crores of rupees, by way of central tax alone.

Tourist marketing has been a fascinating subject for research purposes Krishna and Govindaswamy[39] have made an extensive study on tourist marketing. According to them, unlike the normal consumer product or service tourism cannot develop. Tourist product is marketed at two levels. (i) The national or regional tourist organisation must promote a marketing campaign to persuade the potential tourists to visit our country or a specific region for which it is responsible and (ii) The various individual firms providing tourist services can be allowed to market their own components of the total tourist product, after the national tourist organisations launch marketing campaigns, in order to persuade potential tourists to visit the country or region of their interest.

Bezbaruah[40] dwells on the current scenario of tourism. Tourism generates tax revenues to the tune of $655 billion. It employees 10.6 per cent of the global work force. It contributes 10.2 per cent to world's GDP. It is the largest industry with $3.4 trillion gross output. Tourism accounts for 10.9 per cent of all-consumer spending, 6.9 per cent of all government spending and also 10.7 per cent of capital investment in the world.

Dharmarajan[41] is of the view that tourism is an instrument for development. The most significant feature of tourism industry is the contribution to sustainable human development through poverty alleviation, employment generation and environmental regeneration in remote as well as backward areas.

Rabindra Seth[42] points out the seven major hurdles to foster tourism growth in India. They are land and land laws, power, telecoms, roads, road transport, airports and aviation policy. The author says that these are the most striking hurdles, facing our tourism industry.

Brij Bhardwaj[43] makes the following remarks about the infrastructure for tourism growth. 'The steps taken so far include grant of export house status to tourism. With this, the tourism industry will get the benefit of special import license, waiver of bank guarantee for imports and income tax exemption for reinvestment in tourism industry which will help in building the infrastructure'.

Cees Goossens[44] focused on the motivational aspects of destination choice behaviour. In a marketing context, a conceptual model using push, pull and hedonic factors was developed for research on evaluation of destination attributes. In this context, tourists are pushed by their emotional needs and pulled by the emotional benefits. Consequently, emotional and experiential needs are relevant in pleasure-seeking and choice behaviour. From an information processing point of view, it is suggested that mental imagery is an anticipating and motivating force that mediates emotional experience evaluations and behavioural intentions. The conceptual model is relevant for managers who want to know the effective and motivational reaction of customers to promotional stimuli.

Simon Wong Chak Keung[45] investigated the tourists' perceptions of hotel frontline employees' questionable job-related behaviour. Tourists were asked to indicate their perceptions on hotel employees' ethics in their service encounters (Front Office, Housekeeping and Food & Beverage). Four dimensions were identified by factor analysis. Listed in a descending order, from "Wrong" to "Not Wrong". They were: 1) Infringement of guests' privacy 2) unethical behaviour; 3) benefiting at the expense of guest-supplementary service and 4) working against company work-rules. Pearson's correlation analysis revealed certain relationships between the four dimensions and six independent attitudinal statements. An attempt was carried out to investigate whether any significant differences existed between the tourists. Demographic variables were analysed using independent t-test and ANOVA with the four identified dimensions. It was found that gender exerted significant difference, while age, education, nationality and purpose of stay, scored differently in some factors. Recommendations to hotel practitioners were given in the areas of protecting guests' privacy, ethical education to employees disciplinary rules, and equitable rewards for catering to tourists needs.

Kuo-Ching Wang, An-Tien Hsieh and Tzung-Cleng Huan[46] identified the critical service features of the group package tour. In many countries, especially in Asia, the group package tour is the mainstream mode of outbound travel. Little effort has been devoted to improve our understanding of the grounded service features of the group package tour. In order to fill this gap and thereby enhance the foundations of group travel theory, this study was conducted. Based on the data, 25 distinct ground service features were identified. At the end, the authors also discussed implications for future systematic investigation model development, and made recommendations for tour operators.

Manjula Chaudhary[47] conducted a research for the purpose of determining pre-and post-trip perceptions of foreign tourists on India as a tourist destination. A gap analysis between expectations and satisfaction levels was made to identify strengths and weakness of Indian tourism-related image dimensions so that necessary efforts could be made to meet the tourists' expectations. Along with the overall comparison of the expectations and satisfaction levels of the total samples, the three groups of tourists (German, British and Dutch) were compared to find whether these segments differed regarding India's image attributes as measured in the study. These three segments were considered important markets by leading travel agencies.

Enrique Bigne et al.,[48] focused on the relationship between the image of a destination as perceived by tourists and their behavioural intentions, and their post-purchase evaluation of the stay. The authors also examined the relationship between quality and satisfaction and between these variables and the tourists' behaviour variables. They placed the accent on a joint analysis of these relationships, using a structural equation model. The results of the empirical study showed that tourism image was the direct antecedent of perceived quality, satisfaction, intention to return and willingness to recommend the destination. The role of image as a key factor in destination marketing was thus confirmed. With reference to the other relationship, on the one hand, it was confirmed that quality had a positive influence on satisfaction and intention to return and that satisfaction determined the willingness to recommend the destination.

Christina and Anadam[49] focused on the mediation of tourism by the host community in the pilgrimage town of Pushkar, India. This study provided a framework for understanding the impact of Western Tourism, in the context of a Hindu religious community. Locally, tourism was perceived as a threat to tradition and religion, even while a segment of the population gained economic benefits. This ambivalence was resolved through three types of rhetoric-exclusionary, political and religious. This strategy of rhetorical resistance, termed here as mediated resistance, allowed the host community to condemn tourists collectively while participating in tourism on individual basis. The theoretical focus of the study was drawn from cultural anthropology, religion and communication of research.

The crux of the argument was that the relationship between tourism and culture was a complex and subtle one, while it was resisted rhetorically. This matrix of culturally-derived rhetorical strategies, which constituted mediated resistance function, to transform an ambivalent society was culturally acceptable to the host community.

Carson[50] considered three aspects of international tourism. First, he examined the contribution that tourism had made to the development process in the third world countries. Secondly, he considered as to what extent this contribution had been real rather than nominal. Thirdly, he examined some of the criticisms of tourism in this process and asked whether or not the criticisms had substance. The author regarded tourism as a viable means of aiding development. In this sense, it was felt that tourism was recognised as having made a substantial contribution to the development process in many third-world countries. Its benefits have been real and are increasingly sought by many such countries. There are problems and areas of concern, but it would be a fiction to deny the reality of tourism's contribution.

John[51] says, "This study examines residents' perceptions towards ecotourism travel, their level of interest in it as form of pleasure travel, and the barriers involved in undertaking this type of tourism activity. "Ecotourism provides one way to help educate the community to protect and conserve the environment through travel, and also to create and maintain a sustainable environment for both residents and tourists. However, a lack of community awareness and positive attitude towards ecotourism and the environment is likely to lead to misrepresentation and abuse of the concept, and further depletion of the environment especially, with mass tourism. It was found that with a sample of Honk Kong respondents, there was a low level of awareness and knowledge of ecotourism. Over half of the respondents were not aware of it and even if they were, they possessed limited knowledge. While most were aware of its environmental aspects, little or no recognition was given to the other aspects of ecotourism, mentioned by Honey (1999). Furthermore, most respondents also expressed indfference towards ecotourism and were unlikely to take such a trip in near future. Implications of these findings were discussed and addressed.

Maneet Kumar[52] highlighted the existence of a great potential in the Himachal state which was still untapped and which provided ample scope for growth. He was of the opinion that an integrated approach encompassing product identification, infrastructure needs and support services could lead the state to make it a paradise for tourists.

Hubb Gayman[53] says that before discussing the parameters of ecotourism success, it is necessary to discuss first parameters of ecotourism itself. Ecotourism has almost as many meanings as the people who use the term. Therefore, it may be more fruitful to accept that there are many forms and degrees of ecotourism, as opposed to dividing the tourism world into eco and non-eco. Proposed here, is a rating system, based on five parameters. Just as hotels and restaurants receive a rating of one-to-four stars, ecotourism attractions could be judged on a system of butterflies, with respect to their environmental policies. The proposed parameters are: reduced impact on environment/environmental sustainability policies, interaction with nature, community involvement and interaction with people, environmental activities, and economic sustainability. We then ask to what extent an ecotourism venture is able to score high on each of the parameters, on a continuous or sustainable basis.

Verma[54] examined the challenges and opportunities of promoting tourism in India. He highlighted the fact that the time had come to promote leisure tourism in addition to cultural tourism. For long, we have sold the Taj Mahal, the Red Fort and the Jama Masjid, the Burning Ghats of Varanasi, our temples, history, culture and classical dances.

Ecotourism is a concept, which is gaining popularity in many developed western countries. India can be an ideal destination for lovers of ecotourism because of its vastness, salubrious climate and plenty of landscapes. The future of tourism belongs to those who have the courage to move away from the beaten track and traditional itineraries.

Santhosh Thampi[55] explains tourism as a major phenomenon of the modern society. Ecotourism is a new concept in tourism, which was originally sparked off by the idea of making harmonious co-existence with nature, a reality once again. This paper explains the characteristics of ecotourism, social, economic, cultural and environmental impact of ecotourism and moderating the impacts. Ecotourism has the potential to alleviate some of the pressures and problems of man tourism, which include environmental stress, economic dependency and societal disruption. Many protected areas in the country have enormous potential for ecotourism. Tourism Department and Forest Department should work together in co-operation and understanding, for the development and management of ecotourism desinations in the country. There needs to be significant attitudinal changes among the policy makers, the private entrepreneurs, tour operators, destination managers, the visitors and the local community, in order to make ecotourism successful.

James Macgregor[56] considers that ecotourism has been promoted as a significant contributor to resource conservation and environmental protection. However, the typical ecotourism trip usually, includes a number of transportation, accommodation and food service components, that are not necessarily environmentally responsible, but which promote sustainable tourism. Nevertheless, the tourism industry is possibly the only industry sector that can avert the constant environmental destruction, caused by such phenomenon as global warning. A concerted effort by all stakeholders in tourism to adopt sustainable tourism policies and practices at the national and international levels could achieve substantial results over the next generation. The Bahamas government, in co-operation with the organisation of American States commissioned the most comprehensive set of sustainable tourism policies ever prepared.

According to Dimblebey[57] a Travel Writer from Dutch "there is no country in the world where you can experience this amazing diversity of food and culture and festivals and the people. It is the natural warmth and immense hospitality of the Indian people that make all the difference.

Katrina Brandon and Richard Margolvis,[58] argue that the distinguishing feature of ecotourism should be that it benefits biodiversity conservation. We prepare a set of five benefits to conservation, which should be evident in any tourism activity, which claims to be ecotourism. These benefits will not happen spontaneously. They will only result from first specifying a clear framework for analysing the linkages between project-level activities and conservation. It identifies a series of steps, which need to be undertaken as part of project design, which help to identify the logical link between the project design cycle and measuring project success. When such methodological rigor is introduced into ecotourism initiatives, there will be a much greater chance for success to be verifiable and measurable in relation to real-world impacts. It can then provide better sources of learning for other projects and places and genuinely benefit biodiversity conservation.

Geoffrey Wall[59] says that ecotourism is an agent of change. Measurement of the impacts of tourism is fraught with similar challenges to those involved in assessing impacts in general and tourism in particular. Research on the impacts of tourism has not been cumulative because of the adoption of an inappropriate paradigm and inadequate attention to the contexts in which impacts occur. It is suggested that aggregated information is more useful than summary measures and the characteristics of useful indicator for measuring impacts and monitoring change are described.

George Wallace[60] discusses a systematic approach to evaluating ecotourism operations in a given locale. It employs a set of six principles as the basis for evaluation. Indicators and standards are site-specific and agreed upon by managers and stakeholders. When possible, tour operators, protected area managers, visitors and local people participate in the evaluation. The paper gives its definition of ecotourism, discusses how the principles and valuative methods are derived and describes the evolution of methodology by looking at ecotour operations in both Brazillian and Ecuadorian portion of Amazon Basin Suggestions are then offered for improving the approach.

Lori Gould[61] looks at the role of ecotourism, in achieving sustainable community development. Since the focus of the paper is on the developing or less developed world, there is a detailed discussion, outlining the differences in sustainability between the two global areas. The purpose of this paper is to specifically examine ecotourism and sustainable community development, with emphasis on the developing world. There are three main focuses (1) to examine the differences in sustainable development between the developed world and the developing or less developed world, (2) to discuss the variety of types of tourism, paying particular attention to the objectives, benefits and drawbacks of ecotourism and (3) to address what role ecotourism plays in sustainable community development in the developing and less developed worlds.

Akash[62] in his article explains that consumer is the important segment of the economic cycle of the country as other developmental activities centre around him. He decides the success or failure of business in competitive economy either by buying or not buying the product. And the performance of organization is purely based on consumer satisfaction. If the organization does not take proper care towards satisfaction of consumers it may adversely impact on the profitability of organization. Hotel industry plays an active role in developing and developed country in increasing employment opportunity and economic status of the country and its earnings during the financial year 2006-07 was Rs.604.32 billion, a growth of 21.27 per cent. The study clearly reveals that most of the customers are not happy with the services of hotel industry. However the success and survival of hotel industry depend upon proper service to customers.

Ajith Kumar Shokla[63] in his paper, explained that tourism has an international market, but marketing strategies need to be built up from the basic marketing inputs, used in domestic tourism. Cultural differences, political differences and geographical differences are a supreme importance in the tourism and travel market. Marketing strategy inputs need to be adjusted to foreign markets. The tourist products require simplification and adjustment to local differences in taste, price and quality levels. Tourist attraction is regarded as central to the successful development of tourism region and the tourism system as a whole. A range of conceptual frameworks can be seen as highly applicable to trends of marketing management in tourist attraction. The current study is relevant to but not conceived within any one of those frameworks. The concern of the present article is to use a diversity of sources to dormant recent business trends of marketing management in tourist attraction.

Yesodha Devi and Kanchana[64] in their article on "A Study on Customer Preference and Satisfaction Towards Restaurants in Coimbatore city" stated that the majority of the consumers have visited different restaurants at different times. So the restaurant owners have to take steps to retain the customers and make them their permanent customers. Majority of the respondents came to know about the restaurants through their friends. Hence, the restaurants can advertise in the local media like Radio, Newspapers, Magazines, etc. to attract more customers. Quality and taste are the two major factors considered by the respondents in selecting a restaurant and so the restaurant owners should not compromise on these aspects at any cost. Customers are more discerning than demanding and they always want to experiment with the money they spend. They look for new endeavours and experiences and it has become a challenge to keep them loyal to a particular eat-out. With rapidly shifting loyalties, customers who are ready to experiment, look for variety and do not have any specific likes or dislikes. The Indian restaurant industry has come of age by diversifying its services and is trying to cater to the Indian taste buds and is staying in the competitive arena amongst international giants and is able to provide better services to the customers.

Gaurav Jaiswal, et al.,[65] in their study on "Customer Preferences Towards Service Industry: A Factorial Study of Restaurants" found that consumers prefer those restaurants that provide the maximum degree of satisfaction. From this study, it has been concluded, that various factors are responsible for affecting the choice of consumers regarding restaurants. Their attitudes and values related to purchase and consumption will be different. The conversion of rural consumers to purchase sophisticated products is a great challenge for the marketers. But this kind ensures a good demand for sophisticated products in the future. Here, the marketers may have to work harder to sell their goods in rural areas, because of the diversity of values and attitudes present in these regions.

Objectives

The main objectives of the study are:

(1) To undertake a comprehensive study of the major tourist attractions in Kanyakumari district.

(2) To study the trends in tourist arrivals and hotel accommodation in Kanyakumari.

(3) To study the demand and supply of hotel accommodation for tourists in Kanyakumari.

(4) To analyse the expenditure portfolio and its determinants of sample tourists.

(5) To examine the tourists' evaluation of hotel facilities and services in Kanyakumari and

(6) To make suggestions and policy recommendations so that tourism industry is general and hotel industry in particular can hope to have a prospective future.

Methodology

The study requires both primary and secondary data. The primary data could be collected from the respondents by the personal interview method. The secondary data required could be gleaned from prestigious journals and reports. Further, to an extent, reliance on the records and official bulletins of the headquarters of the Tourism Department, Kanyakumari and Office of the Assistant Director of Statistics, Kanyakumari would also be necessary.

Sample Design

In order to assess the development of tourism in Kanyakumari the researcher has adopted stratified random sampling method and the data are collected with the help of tourist information centre in Kanyakumari. For analytical purposes, 500 tourists are targeted as sample tourists and the samples are stratified into two categories namely domestic and foreign tourists. Out of 500 sample tourists, 348 (69.60 per cent) belong to domestic tourists group and the remaining 152 (30.40 per cent) belong to the foreign tourist group and all the sample respondents are randomly selected.

In Kanyakumari 65 hotels are identified as hotels approved by Tourist Information Centre of Department of Tourism, Ministry of Tourism, Government of India. Thus the sample population for the study is 65. The researcher has adopted census sampling method on hotels. All 65 hotels were targeted. Out of these 65 samples 20 hotels are star hotels ranging between 1 to 3 stars the rest were non-star hotels. At the time of data collection all the star hotels responded well and there was 100 percent response. However, as far as non-star hotels are concerned only 30 hotels out of 45 responded, with a response rate of 66.67 percent. In total the researcher collected data from 50 hotels out of 65 hotels with the overall response rate of 76.92 percent.

Collection of Data

On the basis of the information gathered, from the experts and officials of tourism development, a well designed pre-tested interview schedule was drafted and used in the field survey to collect primary data. Before undertaking the main survey, a tentative interview schedule was prepared and administered to 25 tourists, in order to test the validity of the interview schedule. It facilitated the removal of the 'non-response' and unwarranted questions and the modified final schedule were prepared on this basis.

The selected tourists were contacted in person and the objectives of the study were clearly explained to them and their co-operation was ensured. The details regarding the time of arrival, departure, number of days / duration of stay, details of hotel accommodation, expenditure and the like marked the questionnaire.

The secondary data were collected from books, journals, newspapers and periodicals, official records of the Department of Tourism, and internet.

Period of the Study

In order to examine the arrivals of the tourists, the arrivals during the period of ten years from 1999-2000 to 2008-09, to taken as secondary data. The required primary data were collected from the tourists and hoteliers during the year December 2008 to November 2009. Thus the study covers a period of ten years from 1999-2000 to 2008-2009.

Tools for Analysis

In order to analyse the trend and growth of tourists' arrival in Kanyakumari, Semi log trend equation has to be fitted.

In order to examine the opinion of the tourists, regarding environment, hotel facilities and services, the weighted average ranking technique has been adopted.

To identify the determinants of the expenditure of tourists, the log linear multiple regression model is to be fitted.

In order to examine the opinion of the tourists regarding booking of rooms and to assess the degree of delightful tourism activity, the Garrett ranking technique has been adopted.

Limitations of Study

A diligent research work done with utmost care is not devoid of limitations. This research work also is not an exception for this. The researcher experienced the following limitations.

1. The first limitation was the non response rate of non-star category hotels. All the star category hotels responded and 66.67 percent of non-star category hotels alone responded. The researcher felt this as a limitation.
2. The time of data collection from tourists' language was a major barrier. The researcher used English as the medium of communication but majority of the

respondents found it difficulty in understanding the questionnaire and naturally there is possibility of collecting data from educated respondents only. These may be a sampling bias.

3. Another limitation is that the researcher has taken the hotels, approved by Tourists Information Centre of Tourism Department and other hotels are not taken for the sampling. The reason behind this is that the hotels are approved by a Government agency from tourism point of view, However, it was observed by the researcher that the tourism department has also availed the services of other hotels also. As such hotels were not approved by any agency or government body, the researcher excluded such hotels. However, a major chunk of tourists also visit such hotels and this is another limitation.

Chapter Scheme

The present study on "Role of Hotel Industry in the Promotion of Tourism" has been divided into seven chapters.

The first chapter introduces the subject and discusses the contribution of tourism industry in Indian economy, market potential of Indian tourism industry in global perspective, laws covering the hotel industry and tourism, statement of the problem, review of literature, objectives of the study, methodology adopted for the present study, limitations and chapter scheme.

The second chapter discusses the hotel industry scenario.

The third chapter deals with the tourist attractions in southern tip of India.

The fourth chapter analyses the trends in tourist arrivals and hotel accommodation.

The fifth chapter discusses the profile of the tourists, expenditure portfolio and its determinants.

The sixth chapter undertakes an analysis of the hotel industry in the study area.

The seventh chapter presents the summary of the findings of the analysis, conclusion arrived at and offers suitable policy implications.

REFERENCE

1. Akash. S.B., "Consumer Satisfaction in Hotel Industry – An Explanatory Study", *The Journal of Business Studies*, Vol.5, No.9, January 2008, p.38.
2. Charles Kaiser and Larry E. Helber, "*Tourism – Planning and Development*", CBI Publishing Company Inc., Boston, Maccachusetts, 1998, p.174.
3. *The Hindu*, Wednesday, October 7, 1992.
4. "A Policy for Tourism", *Commerce*, Vol.143, No.3706, May 29, 1980, p.7.
5. Kumar B. Dass and Mohanty.P.M., "Profile of International Tourism in India", *Southern Economist*, Vol.29, No.13, August 15, 1992, p.26.
6. *The Hindu*, Thursday, October 22, 1992, p.10.
7. Ministry of Information and Broadcasting, *India Year Book*, Publication Division, Government of India, New Delhi, 1990, pp.629-631.
8. *Ibid.*, p.156.
9. *Ibid.*, p.156.
10. *Ibid.*, pp.156-158.
11. Jagmohan Negi, *Hotel and Tourism Laws*, Frank Bros & Co., 2001, pp.5-6.
12. Saman Khan, "Market Potential of Tourism Services in India", *South Asian Journal of Socio-Political Studies*, Vol. 9, No.2, January-June, 2009, p.155.
13. Pangi, "Goa Aman and Diu: Tourism Promotion Authority", *Commerce*, Vol.131, No.3352, August 16, 1995, pp. 85-87.
14. Kunal Chellopedhyay, "Marketing Tourism Product: A Consumer Travel Decision Approach", *The Asian Economic Review*, 1985.
15. Francesco Frangialli, "Five Challenges for International Tourism up to the Turn of the Century", *Monthly Commentary – Blue Supplement*, Vol. XXXV, No.11, June 1994, p.6.
16. Vivek Sharma, "Tourism: It's Socio-Economic Importance", *Southern Economist*, Vol.24, No.14, November 15, 1985, p.11.
17. Shivashankar Bhat K., "Promoting Indian Tourism", *Southern Economist*, Vol.29, No.1, May 1 1990, pp.23-25.
18. Roy P.R., "Focus on Tourism, Blue Supplement to the Monthly Commentary of India", *Economic Conditions of Indian Institute of Public Opinion*, Vol. XXXI, No.10, May 1990, pp. I-II.
19. Sharma G., "Tourism Industry Needs Revamp", *Southern Economist*, Vol.29, No. 3, May 15 and June 1, 1990, pp.3-4.

20. Shivshankar Bhat K., "Promoting Indian Tourism", *Southern Economist*, Vol.29, No.1, May 1990, pp.23-25.
21. Joseph K.V., "Tourist Market of Kerala", *Yojana,* Vol.35, No.11, November 16-30, 1990, pp.27-28.
22. Joseph B.K.V., "Extent of Demand for the Tourist Product of Kerala", *Southern Economist*, Vol.30, No.12, October 15, 1991, pp. 17-20.
23. Singh L.P., "Tourism Marketing in India – Problems and Prospects", *Southern Economist*, Vol.29, No.18, January 1991, pp. 17-18.
24. Kumar B. Dass and Mohanty P.M., "Profile of International Tourism in India", *Southern Economist*, Vol.31, No.8, August 15, 1992, pp.21-23.
25. Selvam M., "Tourism: Social Impacts", *Kisan World*, Vol.20, No.4, April 1993, pp.49-51.
26. Ritu Galati, "Tourism in Uttaranchal – Prospects and Problems", *Yojana,* Vol.37, No.19, October 1993, pp. 17-18.
27. Veera Sekaran R., "Significance of Tourism in India", *Southern Economist*, Vol.32, No.9, September 1993, p.4.
28. Padmanabha Rao R.A., "Tourism – Medium of Social and Cultural Development", *Yojana,* Vol.40, No.11, November 16-30, p.37.
29. Ameen A.M. Al-Momani, "Tourism Development – Expectations and Apprehensions", *Monthly Commentary*, Vol.XXXVI, No.11431, June 1995, pp.23-25.
30. Sarngadharan M., "Needs for Promotion of Tourism in India", *Employment News Weekly*, Vol.XX, No.12, New Delhi, June 17-23, 1995, p.1.
31. Vijaya Kumar A., "New Strategy for Indian Tourism Industry", *Southern Economist*, Vol.37, No.11, October 1, 1998, pp. 18-19.
32. Indar Sharma, *Travel Industry in the Year 2000.*
33. Vijaya Kumar T and Bhagavan M.K., "Tourism the Potential", *Yojana*, Vol.2, No.15, December 1992, pp.11-13.
34. Amean A.M. Al Momans, "Tourism Development – Expectations and Apprehensions", *Monthly Commentary*, Vol.XXXVIII, No.10 & 431, June 1995, pp.23-26.
35. Shrutidhar Paliwal, "Promoting Environment-Friendly Tourism", *Monthly Public Opinion Surveys*, Vol.XLII, No.4, January 1999, p.30.
36. John M.I., "Environmental Economics and Its Importance", *Southern Economist*, Vol.35, No. 4, June 15, 1996, pp.8-10.

37. Singa S.L.N., "The World Bank Atlas, World Profile People, Economy and Environment", *Southern Economist*, Vol. 35, No.14, November 15, 1996, pp.1-5.

38. Dharmarajan S. and Rabindra Seth, "Hotel Industry Persisting Shortage of Rooms", *The Hindu Survey of Indian Industry*, 1997, pp.425-427.

39. Krishna R.K and Govindaswamy M., "Marketing in Tourism", *Southern Economist*, Vol.36, No.22, March 15, 1998, pp. 10-12.

40. Bezbaruah M.P., "Tourism – Current Scenario and Future Prospects", *Yojana*, Vol.43, No.8, August 1999, p.7.

41. Dharmarajan S., "Tourist – An Instrument for Development", *Yojana*, Vol.42, No.6, June 1998, p.19.

42. Rabindra Seth, "Tourism: Problems and Prospects", *Yojana*, Vol.43, No.8, August 1999, pp.21-24.

43. Brij Bhardwaj, "Infrastructure for Tourism Growth", *Yojana*, Vol.43, No.8, August 1999, p.31.

44. Cees Goossens, A Study on "Tourism Information and Pleasure Motivation", *Annals of Tourism Research*, Vol. 27, No.321, 2000, pp.301-321.

45. Simon Wong Chak Keung, "The Study on Tourists' Perceptions of Hotel Frontline Employees' Questionable Job-Related Behaviour", *Tourism Management*, Vol.21, No.10, 2000, pp.121-134.

46. Kuo-Ching Wang, An-Tien Hsieh, Tzung-Cheng Huan, "Critical Service Features in Group Package Tour: An Exploratory Research", *Tourism Management*, Vol.21, No.10, 2000, pp.177-189.

47. Manjula Chaudhary, "India's image as a Tourist Destination-Perspective of Foreign Tourists", *Tourism Management*, Vol.21, No.10, 2000, pp.293-297.

48. Enrique Bigne J. and Isabel Sanchez M., "Tourism Image, Evaluation Variables and after Purchase Behaviour: Inter-relationship", *Tourism Management*, Vol. 22, No.11, 2001, pp.607-616.

49. Christina A. Joseph and Anadam P. Kavoori, "Mediated Resistance-Tourism and Host Country", *Annals of Tourism Research*, Vol. 26, No.4, 2001, pp.998-1007.

50. Carson Jenkins, *Tourism in Third World Development – Fact or Fiction*, Deep and Deep Publications Private Limited, New Delhi, 2001, pp.88-99.

51. John, A.P. and Dora Pang, "*Community Perceptions of Ecotourism*", www.ecotourism.org., 2002.

52. Maneet Kumar, *Tourism Today - An Indian Perspective*, Kanishka Publishing House, New Delhi, 2003, pp.127-139.

53. Hubb Gayman, *"Five Parameters of Ecotourism"*, www.environment_yale.edu., June 2003.

54. Verma G.C., *Tourism in Indian Context: Experiences and challenges*, Deep and Deep Publications Private Limited, New Delhi, 2004, pp.144-148.

55. Santhosh P. Thampi, "Ecotourism – Concept and Impacts", *Review of Social Sciences*, Vol. V, No. 1, January-June, 2004, pp. 64-70.

56. James Macgregor, *"Developing a National Sustainable Tourism Strategy: Going Beyond Ecotourism to Protect the Planets Resources"*, www.ecotourism.org., 2004.

57. Dimblebey, "Wooing the Global Hopping Tourist," *The Hindu*, February 17, 2005, p.8.

58. Katrina Brandon and Richard Margolvis, *"The Bottom: Getting Biodiversity Conservation Back into Ecotourism"*, www. ecotourism.org., 2005.

59. Geoffrey Wall, *"Ecotourism: Change Impacts and Opportunities"*, www.environmet_yale.edu., 2005.

60. George N. Wallace, *"Towards a Principle Evaluation of Ecotourism Ventures"*, www.environment_yale.edu., 2005.

61. Lori A. Gould, *"Ecotourism and Sustainable Community Development"*, www.environment_yale.edu., 2005.

62. Akash G.B., "Customer Satisfaction in Hotel Industry – An Explanatory Study", *The Journal of Business Studies*, Vol.5, No.9, January 2008, pp.38-44.

63. Ajith Kumar Shokla, "Trends of Marketing Management in Tourist Attraction", *Indian Journal of Marketing*, Vol.xxxix, No.5, May 2009, pp.28-34.

64 Yesodha Devi .N and Kanchana V.S., "A Study on Customer Preference and Satisfaction Towards Restaurants in Coimbatore city", *Indian Journal of Marketing*, Vol.xxxix, No.10,October, 2009, pp.56-63.

65. Gaurav Jaiswal, Praveen Sahu and Manita Matharu, ""Customer Preferences Towards Service Industry: A Factorial Study of Restaurants", *Indian Journal of Marketing*, Vol.xxxx, No.1, January 2010, pp.34-48.

CHAPTER

2

Hotel Industry—A Scenario

Introduction

The Hotel Industry comprises a major part of the Tourism industry. Historically viewed as an industry, providing luxury service valuable to the economy only as a foreign exchange earner, the industry today contributes directly to employment (directly employing around 0.15 million people), and indirectly facilitates tourism and commerce. Prior to the 1980s, the Indian hotel industry was a slow-growing industry, consisting primarily of relatively static, single-hotel companies. However, the Asia, held in New Delhi in 1982, and the subsequent partial liberalization of the Indian economy generated tourism interest in India, with significant benefits accruing to the hotel and tourism sector, in terms of improved demand patterns. Growth in demand for hotels was particularly, high during the early 1990s, following the initiatives taken to liberalize the Indian economy in FY1991, as per the recommendations of the International Monetary Fund (IMF). The euphoria of the early 1990s, prompted major chains, new entrants and international chains to chalk out ambitious capacity additions, especially, in the metropolitan cities. However, most of these efforts were directed towards the business travellers and foreign clientele.

In recent years, the hotel sector has grown at a faster rate than GDP. As a result, the share of hotels and restaurants in GDP, at current prices, has increased from 1.2 percent in FY2000 to 1.5 percent in FY2005. In constant (1999-2000) prices, the GDP from hotels and restaurants has increased from Rs. 222.65 billion in FY2000 to Rs. 335.49 billion in FY2005. As a result, the share of hotels and restaurants in total GDP, at constant prices, has increased from 1.24 percent in FY2000 to 1.40 percent in FY2005.

Hotel Industry in India

Over the last decade and half, the mad rush to India for business opportunities has intensified and elevated room rates and occupancy levels in India. Even budget hotels are charging USD 250 per day. The successful growth story of 'Hotel Industry in India' is second only to China in Asia Pacific.

Hotels in India have about 1, 10,000 rooms. According to the tourism ministry, 4.4 million tourists visited India last year and at current trend, demand will soar to 10 million in 2010 - to accommodate 350 million domestic travellers. Hotels in India have a shortage of 1,50,000 rooms, fueling hotel room rates across India. With a tremendous pull of opportunity, India is a destination for hotel chains looking for growth. According to the data relating to WTTC, India, India ranks 18th in business travel and will be among the top 5 in this decade. Sources estimate, that demand is going to exceed supply by at least 100 percent over the next 2 years. Five-star hotels, in metro cities, allot the same room, more than once a day to different guests, receiving almost 24-hour rates from both guests against 6-8 hours usage. With demand-supply disparity, Hotel in India room rates are most likely to rise 25 percent annually and occupancy to rise by 80 percent, over the next two years. 'Hotel Industry in India' is eroding its competitiveness as a cost effective destination. However, the rating on the 'Indian Hotels' is bullish. 'India Hotel Industry' is adding about 60,000 quality rooms, currently in different stages of planning and development and would be ready by 2012. MNC Hotel Industry giants are flocking India and forging joint ventures to earn their share of pie in the race. Government has approved 300 hotel projects, nearly half of which are in the luxury range. Sources say, that the manpower requirements of the hotel industry will increase from 7 million in 2002 to 15 million by 2010.

With the USD 23 billion software service sector pushing the Indian economy skywards, more and more IT professionals are flocking to Indian metro cities. Hotel Industry in India is set to grow at 15 percent a year. This figure skyrocketed in 2010, when Delhi hosted the Commonwealth Games. Already, more than 50 international budget hotel chains are moving into India to stake their turf. Therefore, with opportunities galore the future the scenario of Indian Hotel Industry looks rosy.

Structure of The Industry

Hotels in India are broadly classified into 8 categories viz five star Deluxe, five-star, four-star, three-star, two-star, one-star, heritage and classified hotels by the Ministry of Tourism, Government of India, based on the general features and facilities offered. The ratings are reviewed every five years. As in December 2005 (latest available figure) there are following number and category of hotels in India.

Table 2.1: Category of Hotels in India

Sl. No.	Categories	Number of Hotels	Number of Rooms
1.	5-Star Deluxe	82	18764
2.	5-Star	92	11332
3.	4-Star	132	9401
4.	3-Star	704	31039
5.	2-Star	587	19031
6.	1-Star	212	695
7.	Heritage	83	2216
8.	Classified	50	5127
	Total	**1932**	**103973**

Source: Ministry of Tourism, Government of India

The table excludes hotels in the unorganized sector that have a significant presence across the country and cater primarily to economy tourists.

Premium and Luxury Segment

This segment comprises the high-end 5-star Deluxe and 5-star hotels, which mainly cater to the business and upmarket foreign leisure travellers and offer a high quality and range of services. The segment accounted for 29 percent of the total hotel rooms in the country in December 2005.

Mid-Market Segment

This segment comprises 3 and 4 star hotels, which cater to the average foreign and domestic leisure traveller. This segment also caters to the middle level business travellers since it offers most of the essential services of luxury hotels without the high costs since the tax component of this segment are lower compared with the premium segment.

Budget Segment

This segment covers 1 and 2 star hotels referred to as 'Budget Hotels'. This category does not offer as many facilities as the other segments but provides inexpensive accommodation to the highly price-conscious segment of the domestic and foreign leisure travellers.

Heritage Hotels

In the past four decades, certain architecturally distinctive properties such as palaces and forts, built prior to 1950, have been converted into hotels. The Ministry of Tourism has classified these hotels as heritage hotels.

Others

At any point of time, applications for classification are usually pending with the Ministry of Tourism because of which such properties remain unclassified. The numbeı of hotel rooms pending classification has declined from historical 15-20 percent to 5 percent of the total rooms available in the recent past.

Key Consumer Segments

The market for the hotel industry can be divided into the following key consumer segments based on the purpose of visit:

The Business Traveller

The Business Traveller is a businessman or a corporate executive, travelling for business purposes. This segment includes corporates, both domestic and foreign, who open offices in the hotel premises during start-ups, corporate executives who make extended stay either for long duration projects or while waiting for permanent accommodation (primarily expatriates) and convention arrivals. While the senior executives usually stay in 5 star hotels, the middle level executives, who are much larger in number, stay in the budget hotels. Corporate Catalyst India-A report on Indian Tourism and Hotel Industry, this segment offers better realizations, as they demand relatively smaller discounts on room rents (about 10-15 percent), use more of the facilities such as PCs, fax multi-media, conference halls, etc. Also, the Food & Beverage (F&B) revenues are better as they usually eat in the hotel itself due to their busy schedules.

The Leisure Traveller

The Leisure Traveller could either be a foreigner or a domestic traveller whose primary purpose of visit is holiday or site seeing. Among non-business foreign tourists, the primary motivation for visiting India is largely cultural attraction followed by conferences and conventions, tourist attractions like beaches, wild life, hill resorts, etc. Usually, leisure travellers are part of a package run by a tour operator. The margins offered by leisure travellers tend to be lower because of two reasons. Namely, they seek higher discounts and also provide less F&B revenues as they usually eat out. The business offered by this segment is highly seasonal and tends to peak during September to March period.

Airline Cabin Crew

Airline Cabin Crew forms another important segment because of the repetitive and guaranteed nature of the business that they provide. Usually, these are a part of an annual contract, whereby, in return for a fixed rate, a certain number of rooms are provided on demand for cabin crews. With discount rates in the range of 40 percent and 50 percent, this represents a low-yield segment for hotels in general.

Major Players in The Indian Hotel Industry

The Hotel Industry mainly has the following major players:

Hotel Chains

They comprise major players including Indian Hotels Company Limited (the Taj Group) and associate companies, EIH Limited (the Oberoi Group), ITC Hotels Limited (the ITC Welcome Group), Indian Tourism Development Corporation (ITDC) and Hotel Corporation of India (HCI) (the latter two being under the Public Sector). Most of these chains had an established presence in one or more metro cities prior to the tourism boom of the 1980s. Subsequent to the tourism boom, these chains aggressively expanded their presence in other locations. The private players among the hotel chains are industry leaders and have well-established brand identities across the different industry segments.

Small Chains

They are companies that have come up after the tourism boom of the 1980s and 1990s. Due to lack of prior experience in the hotel industry, these players have preferred to opt for operating/management arrangements with international players of repute. Some of the companies in this category are Hotel Leela Venture (with Kempinski), Asian Hotels (Hyatt International Corporation), Bharat Hotels (formerly with Holiday Inn and Hilton and now with Intercontinental). As late entrants, most of these hotel companies have fewer properties, compared with the big chains. However, most of these players have initiated expansion plans during the late 1990s.

Public Sector Chains

ITDC and HCI boast of some of the best locations in major cities but are relatively underperformers, as compared with their private sector counterparts.

International Hotel Chains

They are also looking at India as a major growth destination. These chains are establishing themselves in the Indian market by entering into joint ventures with Indian partners or by entering into management contracts or franchisee arrangements. Some of the players who have already entered or plan to enter the Indian market include Marriott, Starwood, Berggruen Hotels and Emaar MGF. Most of these chains have ambitious expansion plans especially, with a strong focus on the budget segment and tier II cities.

Localized Hotel Companies

They mainly comprise early entrants who have an established localized presence and who preferred not to expand during the tourism boom but focus on building and catering to a loyal customer base. Corporate Catalyst India - A report on Indian Tourism and Hotel Industry.

Profiles of Some of The Major Players in The Hotel Industry

The profile of major players in the hotel industry like Indian Hotels Company, Sheraton Corporation, Leela Group, Bharat Hotels Group, Oberoi Group, Ashok Group, Hotel Corporation of India and Jaypee Hotels Ltd., is given below.

The Indian Hotels Company

The Indian Hotels Company and its subsidiaries are collectively known as Taj Hotels, Resorts and Palaces, recognised as one of Asia's largest and finest hotel company. Incorporated by the founder of the Tata Group, Jamsetji .N Tata, the company opened its first property, The Taj Mahal Palace Hotel, Bombay, in 1903. The Taj, a symbol of Indian hospitality, completed its centenary year in 2003. Taj Hotels Resorts and Palaces comprises 59 hotels at 40 locations across

India with an additional 17 international hotels in the Maldives, Mauritius, Malaysia, the United Kingdom, the United States of America, Bhutan, Sri Lanka, Africa, the Middle East and Australia. The company has had a long-standing commitment to the continued development of the Indian tourism and hospitality industry. From the 1970s through the 1990s, the Taj has played an important role in launching several of India's key tourist destinations. Working in tandem with the Indian government, the Taj developed resorts and retreats while the government developed roads and railways to India's hidden treasures.

ITC/Sheraton Corporation

ITC's Hotel division was launched on October 18, 1975, with the opening of its first hotel - Chola Sheraton in Chennai. ITC - Welcomgroup Hotels, Palaces and Resorts, is today one of India's finest hotel chains, with its distinctive logo of hands folded in the traditional Namaste is widely recognised as the ultimate in Indian hospitality. Each of the chain's hotel pays architectural tribute to ancient dynasties, which ruled India from time to time. The design concept and themes of these dynasties play an important part in their respective style and decor. With more and more hotels being added at strategic destinations, the group has joined hands with the Sheraton Corporation to strengthen its international marketing base. A successful marketing franchise for almost 25 years now, there are currently 10 ITC – Welcomgroup Sheraton hotels, and more in the pipeline.

The Leela Group

Founded in 1957 by Capt. C.P. Krishnan Nair, the Rs.4.5 billion Leela Group is engaged in the business of ready-made garments and luxury hotels and resorts. The Leela Kempinski, Mumbai and The Leela, Goa are two of the best hotels in India, and have also won considerable international acclaim. To have achieved this in 12 short years is nothing short of remarkable. Recently in 2001 Capt. Nair fulfilled his longstanding dream of constructing a palace hotel in the garden city of Bangalore. The Leela Palace Kempinski, Bangalore is built in art- deco style, recreating the grandeur of The Mysore Maharaja's Palace. It is set amidst 8 acres of landscaped garden and waterfalls. It is a palace with the heart of a modern hotel. Corporate Catalyst India A report on Indian Tourism and Hotel Industry, Its 254 rooms are opulently furnished and are befitting royalty. The newest addition The Leela Kovalam is Kerala's largest resort, built on a rock –face, cradled between two wide sweeping beaches with a stunning view of the famous Kovalam coastline.

The Bharat Hotels Group

The Bharat Hotels group is a major player in India's tourism and hotel sector. It operates its hotels under 'THE GRAND' banner and its present portfolio of hotels incorporates fourteen luxury hotels in the five-star Deluxe segment. These include Intercontinental 'The Grand' hotels in New Delhi, Mumbai, Goa & Srinagar and The Grand Ashok, Bangalore, The Grand Laxmi Vilas Palace, Udaipur and The Grand Temple View, Khajuraho. Additionally, the hotels opened in 2008-09 are - The Grand Great Eastern, Kolkata, The Grand Jaipur, The Grand Resort, Bekal, The Grand Ahmedabad, The Grand Chandigarh, The Grand Noida and The Grand Fort, Dubai. In 2009, the company had opened hotels in Hyderabad, Amritsar and other key locations.

The EIH Limited (The Oberoi Group)

Asian elegance is the key to running hotels, if you ask EIH (better known as The Oberoi Group). The company owns and operates about 20 luxury hotels, about 10 mid-range hotels, and two inland cruises; The Oberoi Group through operating primarily in India, is also in Australia, Egypt, Indonesia, Mauritius, and Saudi Arabia. Most of the company's luxury properties bear the Oberoi banner. The company in 2004 joined forces with Hilton International, to rebrand most of its mid-range hotels as Trident Hiltons (the former Oberoi Towers is now known as the Hilton Towers, Mumbai). The Oberoi Group also operates luxury cruises of the Nile River and India's Kerala region.

India Tourism Development Corporation / The Ashok Group

India Tourism Development Corporation was established in 1966 as an autonomous public sector corporation, entrusted with the task of helping develop tourism infrastructure and promoting India as a tourist destination. The ITDC Ashok Group of hotel chains manages some of the best five star and luxury tour hotels in the Indian hospitality industry. The hotels run by the ITDC Ashok Group of hotel chains, may be divided into different categories, namely elite hotels, comfort hotels and classic hotels. The ITDC Ashok Group of hotel chains manages 33 hotels in 26 different tourist destinations all over India. The management of Ashok Group believes in offering the best in the hospitality industry and the staff in each of the hotels run by the group are especially, trained to be courteous and efficient. The Ashok Group of hotel chains, boasts of running some of the best hotels in the Indian hotel industry. The hotels that are a part of the elite and classic category of the ITDC Ashok Group are the Ashok Hotel in New Delhi, the Kovalam Ashok Beach Resort in Kovalam, Kerala, the Agra Ashok in Agra, Hotel Jaipur Ashok in New Delhi and the Qutab Hotel, Corporate Catalyst India A report on Indian Tourism and Hotel Industry, New Delhi. Most of the hotels managed by the ITDC Ashok Group have had the privilege of playing host to several international and national dignitaries.

The Hotel Corporation of India

The Hotel Corporation of India Limited is a public limited company, wholly owned by Air India Limited and was incorporated on July 8, 1971 under the Companies Act, 1956, when Air India decided to enter the Hotel Industry, in keeping with the prevalent trend among world airlines. The objective was to offer to the passengers a better product, both at the International Airports and at other places of tourist interest, thereby also increasing tourism in India.

Jaypee Hotels Limited

Jaypee Hotels Limited is primarily engaged in the ownership and operation of hotels in India. The company owns three Five Star Deluxe Hotels, namely Jaypee Palace Hotel at Agra, and Jaypee Vasant Continental and Jaypee Siddharth Hotel at New Delhi. It also manages the operation of the hotels Jaypee Residency Manor at Mussoorie and Jaypee Green Resorts. In addition, Jaypee Hotels have a hand in construction operations. The company is headquartered in New Delhi, India. Jaypee Hotels Limited is a subsidiary of Jaiprakash Associates.

Indian Hotel Industry Survey 2008-09

The Federation of Hotel & Restaurant Association of India (FHRAI) collects information from its members through a questionnaire for its annual Indian Hotel Industry Survey, which is analysed and presented in a report. For the year 2008-09, FHRAI received information from 1168 members. Based on FHRAI's 2008-09 survey, information on various aspects of hotel industry in India, like profile of an average hotel, average number of employees per hotel, and Guest Analysis is presented in the below tables.

Room Profile of an average Hotel for the year 2008-09

Table 2.2 shows the room profile of an average hotel for the year 2008-09. Most of the rooms in all categories of hotels were air-conditioned.

From the above table it is observed that the average of the number of single air conditioned rooms in India is 3.9 percent, double 38.7 percent and suites 4.8 percent. In non-air conditioned rooms, single rooms constitute 0.8 percent, double 6.0 percent and suites 0.6 percent.

Table 2.2: Typical Room Profile of an average Hotel for the year 2008-09

(Percentage)

Sl. No.	Composition		5 Star Del-uxe	5 Star	4 Star	3 Star	2 Star	1 Star	Heri-tage	Other	All India Aver-age
1.	Number of responses		30	47	74	447	298	88	39	145	1168
2.	Air conditioned rooms	Single	21.2	23.1	7.2	3.0	2.1	0.9	0.4	1.3	3.9
		Double	132.8	110.8	72.2	42.6	22.5	14.3	25.2	18.1	38.7
		Suites	27.1	8.4	9.7	5.0	2.6	1.6	9.0	1.8	4.8
3.	Non-Air conditioned rooms	Single	0.0	0.0	0.0	0.6	1.0	2.2	0.3	1.3	0.8
		Double	0.0	0.7	3.6	4.3	8.3	10.3	2.9	8.8	6.0
		Suites	0.0	1.6	0.3	0.3	0.9	0.4	0.6	0.6	0.6
	Total Average rooms		**181.1**	**144.6**	**92.9**	**55.8**	**37.3**	**29.6**	**38.3**	**31.9**	**54.7**

Source: Indian Hotel Industry Survey 2008-2009, FHRAI

Average Number of Employees per Hotel for the year 2008-09

The average number of employees per hotel for the year 2008-09 is classified under three categories namely Manager, supervisors and staff and are given in the table 2.3.

Table 2.3: Average Number of Employees per Hotel for the year 2008-09

(Percentage)

Sl. No.	Composition		5 Star Del-uxe	5 Star	4 Star	3 Star	2 Star	1 Star	Heri-tage	Other	All India Aver-age
1	2	3	4	5	6	7	8	9	10	11	12
1.	Number of responses		28	47	68	398	265	78	35	96	1015
2.	Managers	Male	40.3	29.6	15.6	6.4	2.5	2.2	4.3	2.3	7.2
		Female	10.1	6.2	2.5	0.8	0.3	0.1	0.5	0.2	1.2

1	2	3	4	5	6	7	8	9	10	11	12
3.	Supervisors	Male	45.1	28.9	17.7	10.1	4.2	3.5	8.6	3.0	9.7
		Female	9.6	3.7	3.0	1.7	0.6	0.3	0.8	0.4	1.5
4.	Staff	Male	215.6	163.9	126.8	63.6	30.7	23.5	54.8	23.5	60.9
		Female	29.8	17.2	10.3	6.4	2.7	2.0	4.5	1.3	6.0
5.	Total Employees		350.5	249.4	175.8	88.9	41.0	31.5	73.5	30.8	86.4
6.	Average Employees/ Room		2.0	1.7	1.9	1.6	1.1	1.1	1.9	1.0	1.6

Source: Indian Hotel Industry Survey 2008-2009, FHRAI

Table 2.3 reveals that the average employee per room for all categories of hotels taken together was 1.6. Among the classified categories, variation was quite low: 1.1 in 1-Star and 2-Star categories and 2.0 in 5-Star Deluxe categories.

Distribution of Hotel Guests by country of origin for the year 2008-09

The following table 2.4 shows the distribution of hotel guests by country of origin for the year 2008-09.

Table 2.4: Distribution of Hotel Guests by country of origin for the year 2008-09

(Percentage)

Sl. No.	Composition	5 Star Deluxe	5 Star	4 Star	3 Star	2 Star	1 Star	Heri -tage	Other	All India Average
1	2	3	4	5	6	7	8	9	10	11
1.	Number of responses	23	32	49	186	79	20	20	8	417
2.	ASEAN*	2.7	4.1	4.5	6.5	4.9	3.3	2.6	8.3	5.2
3.	Australia	3.7	2.4	3.4	3.4	4.1	4.4	3.6	3.7	3.5
4.	Canada	2.3	1.8	4.3	3.4	3.3	4.5	2.1	13.9	3.5
5.	Caribbean	0.4	0.2	0.6	0.6	0.7	0.8	0.2	0.0	0.6
6.	China	1.6	1.8	3.0	5.3	3.2	6.8	0.9	2.6	3.9
7.	France	3.6	6.2	7.0	5.8	4.6	5.9	19.1	6.8	6.3
8.	Germany	8.9	5.9	8.0	6.5	5.1	6.7	11.7	6.6	6.8

1	2	3	4	5	6	7	8	9	10	11
9.	Japan	3.3	4.2	6.1	4.9	3.2	5.4	4.0	3.9	4.6
10.	Middle East	2.2	2.0	3.4	4.0	3.6	4.4	1.8	1.3	3.5
11.	Other	9.1	10.1	7.8	9.6	9.3	5.9	5.5	9.3	9.0
12.	European Russia	3.5	3.2	3.1	3.8	2.1	2.2	0.7	2.6	3.1
13.	SAARC**	2.4	3.8	2.9	6.0	11.7	6.2	2.4	11.8	6.2

Source: Indian Hotel Industry Survey 2008-2009, FHRAI

It is seen from the above table that the highest number of guests were from Germany, constituting 6.8 percent, followed by France 6.3 percent and other countries constituting 9.0 percent. The lowest number of guests were from the Caribbean constituting 0.6 percent.

Hotels in Tamil Nadu

The beautiful destination of Tamil Nadu has always been the foremost choice for the travellers because of the beautiful sites and places of interest in the state. Tamil Nadu is a beautiful state that has several cultural importances. A large number of travellers from all over the country visit Tamil Nadu to explore its beauty and richness. To accommodate the travellers visiting the state, there are a large number of hotels in Tamil Nadu.

All the major cities of Tamil Nadu have hotels of various categories, to accommodate all classes of the toutists. Hotels are in all major cities of the state, which include Chennai, Maduari, Ooty, Kodaikanal, Kanyakumari, Pondicherry, Thanjavur, Palani, Vellore, Tuticorin, Salem, Nagercoil, Namakkal, Rameswaram, Coimbatore, Tirupur, Trichy, Karur, Chidamabaram and other destinations. The Tamil Nadu hotels are built, keeping in mind the individual preferences, requirements, budget and taste of the travellers.

There is no dearth of accommodation for travellers in Tamil Nadu. The hotels offer world-class accommodation facilities and services. The various categories of hotels in Tamil Nadu, include heritage hotels, airport hotels, business hotels, boutique hotels, five star hotels, four star hotels, budget hotels, discount hotels, cheap hotels, resorts and guest houses.

There are various government approved hotels as well in this state.

Major Hotels in Tamil Nadu

Some of the major hotels in Tamil Nadu are Taj Connemara in Chennai, Taj Coromandel in Chennai, Hotel Saradharam in Chidambaram, Hotel Sangam in Tanjore and Kanyakumari, Kodai International in Kodaikanal, Hotel Golden Sand and Beach Resort in Mamallapuram, Taj Garden Retreat in Madurai, Hotel Singaar International, Hotel Sparsa in Kanyakumari, The Monarch Hotel in Ooty and Hotel Heritage Inn in Coimbatore.

The following table 2.5 shows the distribution of hotels in Tamil Nadu based on the place and the number of rooms in them.

Table 2.5: Hotels in Tamil Nadu

Sl. No.	Places	No. of Hotel	No. of Rooms
1	2	3	4
1.	Avinashi	5	120
2.	Batlagundu	3	60
3.	Chennai	285	12810
4.	Chidambaram	6	175
5.	Coimbatore	35	2128
6.	Colachel	2	55
7.	Gobichettipalayam	3	62
8.	Coonoor	7	111
9.	Courtallam	5	197
10.	Darasuram	2	45
11.	Dindigul	8	190
12.	Erode	12	235
13.	Gudalur	8	205
14.	Hosur	10	215
15.	Hogenakkal	4	62
16.	Kanchipuram	13	354
17.	Kanathur	3	71

1	2	3	4
18.	Kanyakumari	65	2255
19.	Kallakurichi	3	65
20.	Kalhatti, Nilgiris	5	85
21.	Karur	7	91
22.	Kolli Hills	3	44
23.	Kodaikanal	18	508
24.	Madurai	25	1120
25.	Mamallapuram	12	1012
26.	Masinagudi	3	58
27.	Namakkal	11	191
28.	Theni	7	231
29.	Palani	5	172
30.	Perambalur	4	61
31.	Pollachi	14	545
32.	Pudukkottai	14	355
33.	Rajapalayam	2	75
34.	Ranipet	4	69
35.	Salem	49	1205
36.	Sriperumpudur	12	397
37.	Tanjore	16	325
38.	Tenkasi	3	82
39.	Trichy	18	395
40.	Tirunelveli	7	185
41.	Tirupur	20	775
42.	Tuticorin	5	315
43.	Udagamandalam	15	674
44.	Valparai	5	210
45.	Vellore	16	315
46.	Virudhunagar	6	172
47.	Vriddhachalam	2	58
48.	Yercaud	6	412
	Total	**793**	**29552**

Source: Administrative Records of Hotels maintained by Ministry of Tourism

Table 2.5 reveals that the highest number of 285 hotels are in Chennai and number rooms are 12810. In Kanyakumari, total number of hotels is 65, and the number of rooms is 2255. The lowest number of hotels in Tamil Nadu are found in Colachel, Darasuram, Rajapalayam and Vriddhachalam.

Hotels in The Study Area

In Kanyakumari, there are 65 hotels functioning properly. Their names are given in the below table 2.6.

Table 2.6: Total Number of Hotels in Kanyakumari

Sl. No.	Names	Sl. No.	Names
1	2	3	4
1.	Hotel Alankar	34.	Hotel Ramshath
2.	Ashoka Lodge	35.	Hotel Rehoboth
3.	Balagi Tourist Home	36.	Hotel Saagar
4.	Bhagavathi Lodge	37.	Hotel Safan
5.	Hotel Bhagya	38.	Hotel Samudra
6.	Bhoobathi Lodge	39.	Hotel Sangam
7.	Hotel Calcutta	40.	Sankar's Guest House
8.	Hotel Cape Residency	41.	Saravana Tourist Home
9.	D.K.V. Lodge	42.	Shiva Tourist Home
10.	Hotel Duruva	43.	Hotel Shivas Residency
11.	Hotel Ganesh	44.	Sea Land Lodge
12.	Ganga & Ganga Annex	45.	Hotel Sebaa Palace
13.	Green Palace	46.	Hotel Singaar International
14.	Gomez Lodge	47.	Subbiah Tourist Home
15.	Gopi Nivas Lodge	48.	Hotel Sun Rock
16.	Hotel Jebasakthi International	49.	Tri Sea Hotel
17.	Hotel Jaas	50.	Triveni Tourist Home
18.	Iamalia Lodge	51.	Hotel Vinanchi Arachi
19.	Jyothi Lodge	52.	Vivekas Tourist Hotel
20.	Sri Pioneer Karthikai Lodge	53.	Yamuna Lodge
21.	Hotel Kanya Residency	54.	Sea View Residency

1	2	3	4
22.	Sri. Krishna Lodge	55.	Hotel Sea View
23.	Kaveri Lodge	56.	Hotel Sparsa
24.	Lekshmi Tourist Home	57.	Hotel Melody Park
25.	Hotel Maadhini	58.	Hotel Sun World
26.	Manickam Tourist Home	59.	Hotel Tamil Nadu
27.	Meenakshi Bhavan	60.	Hotel Siva Murugan
28.	Morning Star Lodge	61.	Hotel Sun Rise
29.	Nageswari Tourist Home	62.	Hotel Kanya
30.	Hotel Narmatha	63.	ALK Shiva Tourist Home
31.	New Cape Hotel	64.	Santhi Residency
32.	N.R.S. Lodge	65.	Hotel Ponmurugan
33.	Parvathi Nivas		

Source: Tourist information centre, Kanyakumari

Table 2.6 shows that the, list of hotels in Kanyakumari.

Profile of Major Hotel Players

The hotel business in Kanyakumari mainly has the following major players.

Hotel Sangam

Established in 1983, Hotel Sangam is situated in the main road of Kanyakumari and the access time from the Kanyakumari Railway station and Bus-stand is walk able distance.

Hotel Sangam is an oasis of comfort and style, situated in the heart of Kanyakumari. With a locale near Kanyakumari Temple, boat jetty, beach and shopping bazaar, this hotel provides a great base to explore the exciting Kanyakumari tourist attractions.

For breakfast, lunch and dinner, the restaurant serves multi cuisine with North Indian and South Indian dishes. Hotel Sangam functions with 25 well furnished, A/C and Non A/C rooms. The restaurant is well known for its delicious preparations of fresh sea foods.

Table 2.7: Hotel Sangam Tariff

Sl. No.	Rooms Type	No. of Rooms	Off Season Rate Rs.	Peak Season Rate Rs.
1.	2 Bedded Deluxe A/c	5	1500	1750
2.	2 Bedded Standard A/c	2	1200	1500
3.	4 Bedded Deluxe A/c	1	2150	2600
4.	2 Bedded Deluxe Non A/c	10	1200	1500
5.	2 Bedded Standard Non A/c	2	875	1000
6.	4 Bedded Deluxe Non A/c	5	1850	2000
7.	Extra Bed A/c Rs. 250 Non A/c Rs. 150	-	-	-
	Total Rooms	**25**		

Source: Primary data

Gopi Nivas Grand

Gopi Nivas Grand is the first hotel from the Sangam Group of Hotels. It was established in 1968. Since then this hotel has been providing wonderful hospitality to the customers.

Table 2.8: Tariff in Gopi Nivas lodge

Sl. No.	Type of Rooms	No. of Rooms	Off Season Rate Rs.	Peak Season Rate Rs.
1.	2 Bedded Standard Non A/c	16	550	1000
2.	2 Bedded Deluxe Non A/c	15	650	1300
3.	3 Bedded Standard Non A/c	12	700	1400
4.	4 Bedded Standard Non A/c	6	800	1600
5.	3 Bedded Standard Non A/c	13	900	1800
6.	Extra Bed Non A/c Rs.150	-	-	-
	Total Rooms	**62**		

Source: Primary data

Gopi Nivas epitomizes a philosophy that still holds true today, providing excellent service and facilities for all tourists at a very moderate charge. Gopi Nivas is located near the seashore and it is located too close to the temple and Vivekananda Rock memorial. The time taken to reach the major tourist attractions present in Kanyakumari, by walk, will be less than five minutes from the hotel.

Gopi Nivas has an awesome appearance and the reception has a combination of both the traditional and corporate look. The lobby is very spacious and the travel kiosk is present near the lobby. Gopi Nivas functions with 62 well furnished, A/C and Non A/C rooms. Deluxe rooms or Standard rooms complemented by amenities including free internet access, free travel solutions and a daily newspaper.

Hotel Samudra

Established in 1992, Hotel Samudra is situated very close to Kanyakumari Bagavathy Amman Temple, Vivekananda Rock Memorial and Tiruvalluvar statue. The speciality of Hotel Samudra is that the Kanyakumari temple tower can be viewed from all the rooms of the hotel. Hotel Samudra has its entrance in the Sannathi Street which is the main place of shopping bazaars where one can purchase all types of traditional items,

Table 2.9: Tariff in Hotel Samudra

Sl. No.	Type of Rooms	No. of Rooms	Off Season Rate Rs.	Peak Season Rate Rs.
1.	2 Bedded Deluxe A/c	11	2000	2875
2.	2 Bedded A/c Executive Suite	3	3900	4600
3.	2 Bedded Standard Non A/c	4	950	1400
4.	2 Bedded Semi Deluxe Non A/c	4	1250	1725
5.	2 Bedded Deluxe Non A/c	10	1500	2300
6.	3 Bedded Deluxe Non A/c	3	1650	2415
7.	4 Bedded Semi Deluxe Non A/c	3	1400	2580
8.	4 Bedded Deluxe Non A/c	3	1850	2875
9.	Extra Bed A/c Rs. 250 Non A/c Rs. 150	-	-	-
	Total Rooms	**41**		

Source: Primary data.

shells, hand made bags etc. Hotel Samudra has 41 well furnished A/C and non A/C rooms. Both the sunrise and sunset can be viewed from the room's balcony itself. The hotel has a spacious car parking, safe guarded by securities.

Triveni Tourist Home

Established in 1995, Triveni Tourist Home is the largest hotel in Kanyakumari sprawling over two acres and having 168 well furnished A/C and non A/C rooms. It is located in the main road and so makes Kanyakumari railway station and Kanyakumari bus stand easy accessible. Triveni tourist home has double bedded rooms, three bed rooms, four bedded rooms and even six bedded rooms. These multi bedded rooms give one an opportunity to stay together with friends and families in a single room, thus making the stay unforgettable. Triveni tourist home has a pure vegetarian restaurant and a multi cuisine restaurant. The parking space available is so large that it can accommodate more than sixty cars at a time.

Table 2.10: Tariff in Triveni Tourist Home

Sl. No.	Type of Rooms	No. of Rooms	Off Season Rate Rs.	Peak Season Rate Rs.
1.	2 Bedded Deluxe A/c	29	1100	1500
2.	4 Bedded Deluxe A/c	27	1850	2600
3.	2 Bedded Deluxe Non A/c	30	900	1200
4.	4 Bedded Non A/c	20	1250	1800
5.	4 Bedded Deluxe Non A/c	9	1550	2100
6.	6 Bedded Standard Non A/c	7	1265	2200
7.	8 Bedded Standard Non A/c	12	2070	3000
8.	12 Bedded Deluxe Non A/c	4	2875	4000
9.	Extra Bed A/c : Rs.250 Non A/c Rs.150 Hall (40 Person Capacity) Non A/c	14	2500	3000
10.	Mini Hall (20 Person) Non A/c	4	1700	2000
11.	Single Bedded Deluxe Non A/c	12	300	500
	Total Rooms	**168**		

Source: Primary data.

Lakshmi Tourist Home

Established in 1989, Lakshmi Tourist Home is the hotel which is situated just behind the beach. Lakshmi Tourist Home has 39 well furnished rooms and all the rooms present in the hotel are sea facing. The hotel has a multi cuisine restaurant which serving you mouth watering sea foods. If are wants to relax mind and body, he can have an ayurvedic massage and the hotel arranges for it. The hotel is present in the eastern side of Cape Comorin and so the guests can experience the live moment of the sunrise. The major tourist attractions such as Kumari Amman temple, Triveni Sangamam, Vivekananda Rock and Thiruvalluvar statue can be easily reached from the hotel.

Table 2.11: Tariff in Lakshmi Tourist Home

Sl. No.	Type of Rooms	No. of Rooms	Off Season Rate Rs.	Peak Season Rate Rs.
1.	2 Bedded Deluxe A/c	3	1200	2000
2.	2 Bedded Executive A/c	2	1950	3000
3.	2 Bedded Standard Non A/c	5	750	1200
4.	2 Bedded Semi Deluxe Non A/c	25	950	1500
5.	3 Bedded Standard Non A/c	3	1150	2400
6.	4 Bedded Standard Non A/c	1	1400	3000
7.	Extra Bed A/c Rs. 250 Non A/c Rs.150			
	Total Rooms	**39**		

Source: Primary data

Hotel Seaface

Established in 1997, it is the hotel in which all rooms are sea facing. It is located in the prime location of Kanyakumari to which all the major tourist attractions are too close. It consists of 56 well furnished A/C and non A/C rooms. Executive rooms are also available. The hotel is situated in such a location that the sea breeze passes to the locality only after crossing Seaview Lodge. The Buffet dinners can be arranged in the beach side, for group bookings. The parking available in the hotel is very spacious. Executive suites are well designed, containing coffee makers and hair driers in the room. The executive suite is provided with a complimentary newspaper and complimentary breakfast. The sunrise and sunset could be enjoyed from the room itself. All the rooms are provided with CTV connections and 24 hours running hot water is available.

Table 2.12: Tariff in Hotel Sea Face

Sl. No.	Type of Rooms	No. of Rooms	Off Season Rate Rs.	Peak Season Rate Rs.
1.	2 Bedded Standard A/c (Road Facing)	21	3200	3450
2.	2 Bedded (Sea Facing) A/c	15	3900	4050
3.	Twin Room (Sea Facing) A/c	5	5400	5600
4.	2 Bedded Executive Suite A/c	5	4600	4750
5.	2 Bedded Deluxe (Sea Facing) Non A/c	10	2500	2750
	Total Rooms	**56**		

Source: Primary data

Parvathi Nivas Lodge

Established in 1980, Parvathi Nivas Lodge is known for its traditional appearance and the rooms present in this hotel

Table 2.13: Tariff in Parvathi Nivas Lodge

Sl. No.	Type of Rooms	No. of Rooms	Off Season Rate Rs.	Peak Season Rate Rs.
1.	2 Bedded Deluxe Non A/c	7	550	1000
2.	2 Bedded Standard Non A/c	7	600	1100
3.	3 Bedded Standard Non A/c	3	750	1300
4.	4 Bedded Standard Non A/c	4	900	1500
5.	Extra Bed Non A/c Rs.150	-	-	-
	Total Rooms	**21**		

Source: Primary data

are in Kerala custom. We can taste Kerala dishes and fresh sea foods in Parvathi Nivas Lodge. Separate hall and kitchen facilities are provided to the guests. This hotel has a very good car parking and it is located in the West car street, Kanyakumari. It has budget rooms that are suitable for the economy type guests.

Hotel SeaView Residency

Established in 2002. Hotel Seaview is a 3 Star Category hotel from the Sangam Group of Hotels. It is the only star hotel which functions with the international standards, in Kanyakumari. The lobby level lawn, in the lap of Bay of Bengal provides a great venue to enjoy the beauty of the landscape and the waterscape with the Vivekananda Rock and 133 feet Thiruvalluvar statue in mid-sea. Hotel Seaview has an exclusive multi-cuisine restaurant which serves a spread of delicious Continental, Chinese and Indian recipes and certainly provides one of the best sea food experiences. In the Wave bar, one can surf on the crest of the waves. Cocktails will keep the guests brave and they again, chill it out at the waves. The

Table 2.14: Tariff in SeaView Residency

Sl. No.	Type of Rooms	No. of Rooms	Off Season Rate Rs.	Peak Season Rate Rs.
1.	2 Bedded A/c Sea Facing (Ground Floor)	10	1500	2400
2.	2 Bedded A/c Sea Facing (First Floor)	15	1750	2400
3.	2 Bedded Standard Non A/c	8	950	1850
4.	2 Bedded Deluxe Non A/c Sea Facing	8	1300	2000
5.	2 Bedded Deluxe Non A/c Sea Facing (Ground Floor)	4	1100	1600
6.	Extra Bed A/c Rs. 250 Non A/c Rs. 150	-	-	-
	Total Rooms	**45**		

Source: Primary data

hotel is well -stocked with a choice of spirits. At the land's end of India, a whole new experience of traditional hospitality and perfect service, is provided here.

The Hotel is built on 3 acres of land and is ideally situated overlooking the confluence of the Arabian Sea, the Bay of Bengal and the Indian Ocean. The hotel consists of 45 double bed rooms and 2 luxury suites, a multi-cuisine restaurant, a well-stocked bar, conference facilities, gymnasium, indoor and outdoor games, court Travel desk, Internet facility and swimming pool. The rooms at Sparsa Kanyakumari have been designed to offer the guests a view of the Bay of Bengal from the eastern wing, the Arabian Sea from the western wing and a breathtaking view of the two seas flowing into the Indian Ocean from the southern wing i.e., the seas and under the stars with a touch of a mesmerism.

Hotel Sparsa

Hotel Sparsa is built on 3 acres of land, is ideally situated opposite to the beach, located on Beach Road, next to Sunset Point in Kanyakumari, approximately 90kms from the Thiruvananthapuram Airport, and 2kms from Kanyakumari Railway Station. There is not much greenery around the hotel except for the cultivated shrubs and gardens. But one can see that a lot of saplings have been planted around the grounds and in a few years the place would look lush with tropical greenery. There are 48 air-conditioned rooms/villas at the

Table 2.15: Tariff in Hotel Sparsa

Sl. No.	Type of Rooms	No. of Rooms	Off Season Rate Rs.	Peak Season Rate Rs.
1	Single bedded Deluxe A/c	20	3000	3375
2	2 Bedded Deluxe A/c	26	4000	4500
3	Executive Suite A/c	2	6000	6750
4	Extra Bed A/c Rs. 500	-	-	-
	Total Rooms	**48**		

Source: Primary data.

Resort which are comfortable and spacious, and come with amenities of Wi-Fi internet connectivity (though chargeable), CTV, Telephone, Tea/Coffee maker, A Fruit basket. The hotel also has a Swimming pool, a Spa, a gym, a meditation center, Travel desk and guide services.

Hotel Singaar International

Hotel Singaar International owned by M/s Singaraya Nadar & Sons, was commenced on 30th December 1998. Hotel Singaar International is the very best and the first hotel with three star facilities at Kanyakumari that covers four acres with panoramic views of the Indian Ocean. Its prime location and superior facilities make it the premier choice for the domestic and international tourists and also for business travellers. Hotel Singaar International has 102 rooms in total, out of which there are 6 air-conditioned suites, 26 air-conditioned Deluxe double rooms with panoramic views of the Indian Ocean and 70 non air-conditioned double rooms, with attached bath, telephone, CTV with 20 channels.

Table 2.16: Tariff in hotel Singaar International

Sl. No.	Type of Rooms	No. of Rooms	Off Season Rate Rs.	Peak Season Rate Rs.
1.	2 Bedded Standard A/c	50	2000	2500
2.	2 Bedded Deluxe A/c	20	2500	3000
3.	2 Bedded Luxury A/c	5	3500	4000
4.	2 Bedded Super Deluxe A/c	5	3800	4300
5.	2 Bedded Standard Suite A/c	4	3900	4400
6.	2 Bedded Deluxe Suite A/c	6	4800	5300
7.	2 Bedded Deluxe Non A/c	12	1150	1450
8.	Extra Bed Non A/c Rs.600 Non A/c Rs. 300	-	-	-
9.	Big Hall (250 Person) Per head Rs. 75/-	2		
	Total Rooms	**104**		

Source: Primary data.

Hotel Sun World

Hotel Sun World is situated in Kovalm Road, Kanyakumari in the south of Tamil Nadu. Its unique and key feature is that it offers all amenities to suit one's needs. It provides instant reservation with all comforts. There is a lounge area with comfortable chairs and soothing music. Both the sunrise & sunset can be enjoyed from the rooms. All rooms are sea facing. The hotel is elegantly designed with amazing space for parking. Hotel Sun World offers an experience that makes staying worthwhile and makes the stay more complete.

This is a small hotel in the sense that there are fewer rooms all with attached bath and well furnished neat and tidy rooms. The rooms have 24 hours hot and cold running water, laundry service, doctor on call if needed, safety locker facilities, Direct dialling telephones, Cable TV, Money Exchange facilities and

Table 2.17: Tariff in Hotel Sun World

Sl. No.	Type of Rooms	No. of Rooms	Off Season Rate Rs.	Peak Season Rate Rs.
1.	2 Bedded Deluxe A/c (Sea Facing)	17	3000	3350
2.	2 Bedded Twin Room Deluxe A/c (Sea Facing)	8	6500	6900
3.	2 Bedded Deluxe A/c (Non Sea Facing)	17	2500	2800
4.	4 Bedded Twin Deluxe A/c (Non Sea Facing)	8	5500	6200
5.	Honeymoon Suite (Full Sea Facing)	4	9000	9500
6.	Super Suite Sun World (Sea Facing)	2	7000	7500
7.	2 Bedded Deluxe Non A/c	5	1500	1800
8.	2 Bedded Twin Deluxe Non A/c	5	3500	3800
9.	Extra Bed A/c Rs.900: Extra Person Rs. 300	-	-	-
	Total Rooms	**66**		

Source: Primary data.

all credit cards are accepted. The other services available at Hotel Sunworld are 24 hours room service, not only in the rooms but in the lounges as well.

Hotel Melody Park

Hotel Melody Park is a two Star hotel located at the Sea face of Kanyakumari (Tamil Nadu, India) overlooking the famous Vivekananda Rock Memorial. This is the ultimate place to stay if one wants to stay in Kanyakumari's best hotel. Melody Park, the two-star hotel is quite close to the Kumari Amman Temple. It provides class facilities like A/C and Non-A/C rooms, Deluxe rooms, suite rooms, conference hall, running hot and cold water, satellite TV, E-mail and internet facilities plus international dialing facility 'MARVELL' Restaurant serves Kerala, North Indian, Chinese and continental food at amazingly reasonable tariff. To strengthen the spirits Marco Polo Bar welcomes with open arms. The roof-top restaurant is sure to add charm to the quite evenings. There are 43 rooms and 3 suites - all sea facing.

Table 2.18: Tariffs in Hotel Melody Park

Sl. No.	Type of Rooms	No. of Rooms	Off Season Rate Rs.	Peak Season Rate Rs.
1.	2 Bedded Special Non A/c	5	650	850
2.	2 Bedded Deluxe Non A/c (Sea View)	4	750	950
3.	2 Bedded Standard A/c	12	1000	1300
4.	2 Bedded Deluxe A/c (Sea View)	8	1500	2000
5.	4 Bedded Twin A/c (Sea View)	8	2500	3200
6.	Executive Suite A/c	3	2750	3500
7.	Executive Deluxe Suite A/c (Sea Facing)	3	3000	3800
8.	Extra Bed A/c Rs.250 Non: A/c Rs. 150	-	-	-
	Total Rooms	**43**		

Source: Primary data.

New Cape Hotel

New Cape Hotel, situated near the sea beach with the railway station hardly 5 minutes away, offers delightful accommodation, service and plenty of modern amenities. The hotel boasts of nicely-adorned rooms, loaded with various amenities reflecting fine sense of aesthetics. The view of the sun is easily seen. The hotel with its pristine location near the marvellous beach provides thoughtfully crafted amenities and services at competitive rates. The services and the modern amenities provided at the hotel are at par with some of the posh hotels in the city. The view from the hotel rooms is a real visual treat to all the discerning travellers.

Table 2.19: Tariff in New Cape Hotel

Sl. No.	Type of Rooms	No. of Rooms	Off Season Rate Rs.	Peak Season Rate Rs.
1.	2 Bedded A/c	10	1200	1800
2.	2 Bedded Non A/c	18	400	800
3.	3 Bedded A/c	2	1500	2200
4.	Suit A/c Deluxe	1	1800	2300
5.	Extra Bed A/c Rs. 250 : Non A/c Rs. 100	-	-	-
	Total Rooms	**31**		

Source: Primary data.

Hotel Tri-Sea

Hotel Tri-Sea offers excellent facilities with all modern amenities. It is the best place for travellers to relax in Deluxe A/C rooms Deluxe non A/C. Rooms. The hotel has a Conference Hall, Restaurant facility etc. Restaurant in Hotel TriSea is the place to enjoy authentic Valencian rice dishes. Hotel Tri Sea Restaurant's special are fresh fish dishes cooked with garlic and pepper. We can taste varieties of North and South Indian dishes like Tandoori dishes.

Table 2.20: Tariff in Hotel Tri-Sea

Sl. No.	Type of Rooms	No. of Rooms	Off Season Rate Rs.	Peak Season Rate Rs.
1.	2 Bedded Standard Back Side Non A/c	5	800	1000
2.	2 Bedded Economy Back Side Non A/c	4	900	1100
3.	2 Bedded Deluxe Sea View A/c	13	1600	1800
4.	2 Bedded Deluxe Sea View Non A/c	5	1100	1300
5.	3 Bedded Deluxe Sea View A/c	14	1900	2200
6.	3 Bedded Deluxe Sea View Non A/c	2	1300	1500
7.	4 Bedded Deluxe Sea View A/c	8	1500	2800
8.	4 Bedded Deluxe Sea View Non A/c	4	1900	2300
9.	5 Bedded Deluxe Sea View A/c	5	3000	3500
10.	5 Bedded Deluxe Sea View Non A/c	2	2200	2500
11.	Suite Room A/c	3	3300	3600
12.	Extra Bed A/c Rs. 250 Non A/c Rs. 100	-	-	-
	Total Rooms	**65**		

Source: Primary data

Hotel Maadhini

Hotel Maadhini offers good accommodation options coupled with efficient and prompt services. Situated very close to the sea beach, all the rooms of this modern hotel are great for sea viewing. Some of the rooms of the hotel are privileged to offer a view of the Vivekananda Rock Memorial. All the 75 well-equipped rooms at the hotel have elegant decor and offer great sea view. They are classified into A/C and non A/C rooms. All the rooms have private balcony and are dotted with numerous contemporary amenities.

Table 2.21: Tariff Hotel Maadhini

Sl. No.	Type of Rooms	No. of Rooms	Off Season Rate Rs.	Peak Season Rate Rs.
1	2 Bedded Deluxe A/c (Sea Facing)	35	950	1900
2	2 Bedded Deluxe Non A/c	30	500	1000
3	4 Bedded Deluxe A/c (Sea Facing)	5	1500	2500
4	4 Bedded Deluxe Non A/c	2	1000	1500
5	5 Bedded Deluxe Non A/c	2	1200	1700
6	5 Bedded Deluxe A/c (Sea Facing)	1	2000	3000
7	Extra Bed A/c Rs. 200 : Non A/c Rs. 100	-	-	-
	Total Rooms	**75**		

Source: Primary data

Hotel Cape Residency

Hotel Cape Residency is surrounded by majestic hills and the plains bordered by colourful sea-shores, fringed with coconut trees and paddy fields. This hotel is located within 5 mins

Table 2.22: Tariff in Hotel Cape Residency

Sl. No.	Type of Rooms	No. of Rooms	Off Season Rate Rs.	Peak Season Rate Rs.
1.	2 Bedded Standard A/c	28	1350	1550
2.	Suite A/c	4	2500	2800
3.	2 Bedded Standard Non A/c	3	700	900
4.	Extra Bed A/c Rs.250: Non A/c Rs.150	-	-	-
	Total Rooms	**35**		

Source: Primary data

walk from the beach, 0.5 km from railway station and 90 km from the airport. The hotel offers well equipped comfortable rooms with all major facilities including cable TV, attached bath, 24 hours room service, running hot and cold water and more. Hotel facilities include restaurant, 24 hours room service, travel desk, free parking, laundry and more. It accepts all major credit cards.

Hotel Tamil Nadu

Hotel Tamil Nadu belongs to the Tamil Nadu Tourism Development Corporation, better known as TTDC. TTDC has done a commendable job in promoting Tamil Nadu, and are promoting the state's enormous tourist potential. These hotels belong to the budget and economy oriented hotels with cheap accommodation facilities. All the rooms in Hotel Tamil Nadu

Table 2.23: Tariff in Hotel Tamil Nadu

Sl. No.	Type of Rooms	No. of Rooms	Off Season Rate Rs.	Peak Season Rate Rs.
1.	2 Bedded A/c	15	1020	1120
2.	Twin Cottage A/c	10	870	895
3.	2 Bedded Non A/c	4	770	870
4.	Twin Cottage Non A/c	4	620	720
5.	2 Bedded Deluxe A/c	7	1120	1120
6.	Super Deluxe Double Room Cottage A/c	4	1620	1620
7.	Youth Hostel Bed Non A/c	10	50	50
8.	2 Bedded Mini Non A/c	5	420	445
9.	3 Bedded Family Room Non A/c	5	630	680
10.	Additional Member A/c	-	100	100
11.	Additional Member Non A/c	-	50	50
13.	2 Bedded Suit A/c	3	1120	1320
14.	6 Bedded Family Non A/c	4	1260	1360
	Total Rooms	71		

Source: Primary data

are standard rooms with an array of facilities. They are attached bathroom, running hot and cold water, hot and cold shower, twin/double beds, TV with satellite channels, Intercom, room service etc. There is a multi cuisine restaurant which serves delicious and lip smacking Indian, Chinese and particularly South Indian cuisine. The dining hall is clean and tidy and the authorities never compromise on cleanliness in the hotel.

The propensity to travel in India has increased. This is evident from the foregoing pages. This chapter elaborated the recent scenario in Hotel Industry both at Global Level and at Indian level. The scenario in Indian level shows the attempts made by the Hotel Industry in fulfilling the expectation of different class of people. In India we are having hotels for ill segments. However, the choice of hotel not depends on economic factor alone, behind this there are other demographic factors which may have the impact on the choice of a particular type of hotel. In the present competitive atmosphere at Kanyakumari hotel management should try to understand their target segment. This chapter has provided at analytical view on the hotel industry in Kanyakumari, from which we can understand the future prospects of the industry.

CHAPTER 3

Tourist Attractions in Southern Tip of India

Introduction

Kanyakumari district enjoys an important place in terms of tourism potential. It can boast of several places of religious, social, cultural, historical and environmental significance in the district. The presence of ancient temples with architectural marvels, carvings, paintings and towers attract a steady stream of tourists throughout the year. The present study is undertaken with a focus on the environmental significance of the tourist spots in particular[1].

The Land's End of India or the point where the three seas meet, is called otherwise with the enhancing nomenclature of Kanyakumari or Cape Comorin. It is one of the most popular tourist spots in the State and indeed, in the country. Part of the fascination is, of course, the fact that it is the very tip of the Indian Peninsula and marks the unique confluence of the Bay of Bengal, the Arabian Sea and the Indian Ocean. One would love to see Cape Comorin during the sacred Chitra Pournami (full moon day in April), when the sun and the moon come face to face at the ends of the horizon. On other full moon days also one can see the sun set and the moon rise almost simultaneously, as if by prior arrangement.

Religious Places

The famous religious places in Kanyakumari district are Church in Kanyakumari, Kumari Amman temple, Suchindrum temple,

Nagaraja temple, St. Xavier's church, Thiruvattar temple, Mondaikadu Bagavathi Amman temple, Peer Mohamed Dargah at Thuckalay and Chittaral rock temple.

Church in Kanyakumari

On the eastern side of the coastal line of Kanyakumari there is a beautiful Church dedicated to the Blessed Virgin Mary known for its

intricate architecture. The 153 feet high central tower of the Church was constructed in 1956. The altar and sanctinary of the old Church date back to the times of St. Xaiver who visited this place in 1543 A.D.[2]

Kumari Amman Temple

Situated overlooking the shore, this temple, is dedicated to the Virgin Goddess, Devi Kanyakumari, a symbol of sanctity and liberty of womanhood. According to a legend, the Devi did penace to marry Lord Siva once upon a time. However, owing to some misfortune, the wedding could not take place and she vowed to remain a virgin (Kanya) sticking on to her decision, despite all appeals. The legend says one can even see the footprints of Devi Kanyakumari on a rock called "Sri Paadha Paarai" in the Vivekananda Rock Memorial Complex. The legend of the place has it that Devi was wearing earnings set with rubies, which were so bright that they could be seen from far at night. Some ships sailing in the sea, mistaking this for the lighthouse, went off course and hit the rocks nearby, and were wrecked. It is in view of this incident that the eastern gate of the temple is kept closed permanently. Male tourists who enter the temple should remove their upper garments, in homage to the female deity.

Suchindrum Temple

It is a famous pilgrim centre, situated about 13 kms from Kanyakumari. The Thanumalayan temple here is a veritable repository of art treasure. The temple has unique, beautiful carvings and sculptures which are rarely to be found elsewhere. The corridor in the Suchindrum temple is one of the biggest corridors in South India. Musical pillars and a huge 18 foot high Hanuman Statue offer ample proof of the artistic skill of the artisans of the past centuries. Inscriptions said to be of the 9th century AD are also found in this temple.[3] The gigantic images of Nandi, locally known as "Makkalai", considered the second biggest in India, can also be seen here. This unique temple is dedicated to Trimurthy Vishnu, Siva and Brahma. The purpose of ones visit to Kanyakumari district will not be accomplished until or unless one visits this temple.[4]

Nagaraja Temple (Nagercoil)

Nagercoil is the headquarters of Kanyakumari district. It is situated 19 kms from Cape Comorin. The Nagaraja temple situated here is unique in many respects. Though Nagaraja (Serpent God) is the presiding deity, the images of the Jain Theerthangaras Mahavira and Parsuanathar are found on the pillars of the temple. The Nagaraja is installed on the ground where it was originally found and the sands are scooped out and given as prasadam to the devotees. The entrance to the temple is reminiscent of the Chinese architecture of a Buddhist Vishara. This is one of the important pilgrimage centres in Kanyakumari district.[5]

St. Xavier's Church

St. Xavier, an outstanding and dedicated priest, visited the coastal areas of Tamil Nadu from Goa. He visited Kottar in Kanyakumari district which was a celebrated commercial centre at that time. During his stay at Kottar he used to worship St.Mary in a small church. While he was at Kottar he averted the invasion of Padagas on the people of Venad and the incident was highly appreciated by the King. In recognition of Xavier's services, the King allotted a land to him for the purpose of constructing a catholic church at Kottar. Interestingly, there was already a church in 1544 in the same place where St. Xavier's church stands now.

The church records show, that the church was built in the year 1600 AD. In the year 1865, the church was enlarged and in 1930, the church was raised to the status of a Cathedral. In

1955, the church was further extended. The church of St. Xavier enjoys repute as a place of miracles for centuries. The annual festival of the Church is celebrated during the month of November/December lasting for 10 days.

Thiruvattar Temple

The temple here is dedicated to 'Adi Kesava Perumal' in the Ananthasayanam posture and is considered one of the 13 sacred places for the Vaishnavas. The inscriptions found in the temple fix its age to the 12th century. Remains of old mural paintings, belonging to a period not later than the 17th century, are seen on the walls of the inner shrine. Wood carvings of exquisite workmanship, adorn some of the structures in the temple. It is about 11 kms north of Thuckalay on the Nagercoil-Kulasekharam road and 46 kms from Kanyakumari.

Mondaikadu Bhagavathi Amman Temple

Mondaikadu is situated on the seacoast 4 kms north-east of Colachel port. This place is famous for its temple dedicated to Bhagavathi Amman. The Amman is in the form of an Ant Hill, about 12 feet in height and with five heads, believed to be growing daily. The annual festival called Mondaikadu kodai is celebrated with great enthusiasm and fanfare during March for 10 days.

Peer Mohamed Dargah at Thuckalay

There is a dargah named "Peer Mohamed Oliyullah Dargah" at Thuckalay, named after the great Philosopher Mohamed Appa, who was born in Tenkasi of Tirunelveli district. After spending sometime in spiritual pursuits in Peermedu of the Kerala State, he came and stayed at Thuckalay. Being a Tamil poet of great eminence, he wrote several books on philosophy. It is said that he laid the foundation stone here for the Padmanabhapuram granite fort. The anniversary of the great philosopher poet is celebrated every year on a grand scale on full moon day in the month of Rajap. Both the people of Kerala and Tamil Nadu attend the celebrations, regardless of their caste, creed and religion.

Chitharal Rock Temple

Chitharal is a small village, situated at a distance of 7 kms from Marthandam and 45 kms from Kanyakumari. It is famous for the rock-hewn temple. The hillock at Chitharal has a cave containing, rock-cut reliefs of sculptures of Thirthankaras and attendant deities inside and outside the cave dating back to 9th century AD. It was converted into a temple for Bhagavathy in the 11th century AD. Cars and vans can reach up to the foot of the hill. Visitors walk for about 10 minutes to reach the temple. The Jain images have been preserved by Central Archaeological Survey of India.[6]

Memorials

The important memorials in Kanyakumari district are Kamaraj memorial, Gandhi memorial, Vivekananda memorial rock, Thiruvalluvar memorial statue and Velu Thambi Dalawah memorial.

Kamaraj Memorial

Regarded as the 'King Maker of India' Kamaraj influenced many political events in the country. From a humble background, he rose to the position of the Chief Minister of Tamil Nadu, through sheer hard work and political acumen. As a tribute to the freedom fighter and 'Perunthalaivar" (meaning great leader) this memorial was constructed where his ashes were kept for the public to pay homage, before immersion into the sea.

Gandhi Memorial

A memorial named Gandhi Smarak Mandir in the Orissa style costing nearly Rs.3 lakhs was constructed on the golden sands of Cape Comorin in the year 1956. It commemorates the immersion of the ashes of the Father of the Nation on 12th February, 1948 at the confluence of the three seas.

At the place where the urn containing the sacred ashes was placed, a big hall has been built. Its central shape is 79 feet high, representing the age of the Mahatma. A striking feature of the massive structure is that it is so constructed that, every year on Gandhi's birthday on 2nd October, the sun rays fall on the exact spot where the urn was displayed before immersion.

Vivekananda Memorial Rock

There are two rocks projecting out of the Ocean. One is 1600 feet away from the southern most end of our holy motherland. This memorial was built in 1970. It is dedicated to Swami Vivekananda, the greatest modern social reformer and saint, India produced in the twentieth century. On 25th December, 1892 Swami Vivekananda swam across the sea and sat in deep meditation on the rock. On this rock a memorial has been constructed in honour of Swami Vivenakanda in the year 1970. A meditation hall is also attached to the memorial. Ferry service is available to reach the memorial.

The Vivekananda Rock Memorial complex consists of four mandapams namely, Sree Pada Mandapam, Vevekananda Mandapam, Subha Mandapam and Dhyana Mandapam.

Thiruvalluvar Memorial Statue

A novel grandeur carved out of a hoary tradition namely 133 feet tall granite statue of Thiruvalluvar, has come up recently almost in mid-sea, off the shore of Kanyakumari. It is to be highlighted that nowhere in the history of world architecture, such a standing human form, fully made of granite has ever been attempted and that too in the midst of the sea waves. The statue is an embodiment of the essence of Tamil Classic "Thirukkural" a collection of pithy verses authored by Saint Thiruvalluvar, which marks the quintessence of the Tamil spirit. The statue located at the confluence of the three great seas, also depicts the great tenets of the Thirukkural namely, virtue, wealth and love.

The imposing 133 feet high statue was erected on a minor rock in mid-sea by Dr.Ganapati Sthapati and his team of around 500 shilpis and other technicians and engineers. The statue is fully made up of granite stones, weighing 7000 tonnes, comprising 3681 pieces of granite boulders, each weighing 3-

8 tonnes. The statue proper, stands 95 feet tall on a pedestal of 38 feet in height and the whole structure has been designed based on the spirit of the poet's great work, "Thirukkural". In the design of the statue, the 38 feet high pedestal depicts the first 38 chapters which deal with the virtue and the statue proper of 95 feet depicts the rest of the 95 chapters, which deal with wealth and love.

There is also a striking feature in this monument which desreves note by modern technicians. The height of the statue is 133 feet, for which a scaffolding work had to be attempted up to a height of 150 feet. In this scaffolding work no steel fabrication was used except the traditional casuarina posts right from the beginning to the end of his mammoth project. The ferry that goes to Vivekananda rock first arrives at Thiruvalluvar statue. After seeing Thiruvalluvar Statue tourists take the next boat to go to the Vivekananda Rock.

Velu Thambi Dalawah Memorial

Thalakulam is a hamlet located in Kalkulam taluk of Kanyakumari district, 30 kms away from Kanyakumari. This place is historically important since it is the birth place of the great revolutionary Velu Thambi Dalawah, a Dewan in the former Travancore State who resisted the British. His ancient home at Thalakulam village was once destroyed by the British. Later on, the house was rebuilt by his nephews, in which some of his personal belongings and personal weapons employed in his battles, against the British are kept.

Thus, Kanyakumari district occupies a place of extraordinary significance as far as its natural environment and history are concerned. The scenic beauty of this unique district has been a major lure for thousands of tourists from far and near. International tourists very often, feel drawn towards these places as the exquisite beauty of the landscape here cannot find a match anywhere. An attempt is made in this chapter to give a vivid portrayal of some of the beaches which have been a major lure for the local and national tourists.

The Fort and Palace

The famous fort and palace in kanyakumari district are circular fort (vattakottai), Udhayagiri fort and Padmanabhapuram palace.

Circular Fort (Vattakottai)

This 18th century fort was built by the Dutch. Overlooking the sea, it is a fine tourist spot. The sea is generally calm here and is suitable for bathing.

Udhayagiri Fort

Built during the regime of King Marthanda Varma (1729-1730 AD) this fort also had a foundry for casting guns. De Lennoy's Tomb is in the fort. He was one of the 24 European prisoners taken by King Marthanda Varma in 1741, when he defeated the Dutch at Colachel. He joined King Marthanda Varma and became a trusted general. He trained soldiers in the European method of combat. Presently, the district administration, with the help of the Department of Forests, has set up a Bio-Diversity park here.

Padmanabhapuram Palace

Padmanabhapuram[7] (City of Lord Vishnu), the ancient historical town is situated 37 kms from Kanyakumari. It was the ancient capital of the erstwhile Travancore (Venad) State from about 1555 AD to the latter half of the 18th century. King Marthanda Varma, the maker of modern Travancore (AD 1729-1758), after ensuring the autonomy of the State, constructed temples, palaces and forts. As a part of his enterprise, the mud fort around Kalkulam palace was demolished and a granite fort was built with four bastions in four corners. In 1744 AD, Kalkulam fort and palace were renamed Padmanabhapuram fort and Padmanabhapuram palace respectively.

The palace is situated at the very centre of the Padmanabhapuram fort with an area of 186 acres of land amidst Veli hills, dales and rivers. The exterior of the palace is simple and unpretentious like other secular and religious architectural specimens of Kerala. The interior is enriched by wood carvings and conspicuous murals. The palace consists of 13 important portions including Mantrasala (council chamber), Manimalika (Clock Tower), Uttupura (Dining Hall), Thaikottaram (Mother palace), Uppirikka Malika (Four storeyed building), Anthapuram (Lady's chamber), the long corridor, Indravilasam Palace, Navarathri Mandapam and Archeological museum etc.

Apart from them, there are many temples inside the fort, among which Sri. Ramaswamy temple, Sri.Subramaniya temple and Saraswathy temple are centres of worship. In the Ramaswamy temple, scenes from Ramayana have been carved on wooden panels.

The Beaches

The very beautiful beaches in Kanyakumari district are Kanyakumari beach, Sothavilai beach, Sanguthurai beach, Thekkuruchi beach, Muttom beach and Thengapattinam beach.

Beach in Kanyakumari

Kanyakumari is noted for its natural beach too. The following are the most sought after tourist heavens.

1. Sunrise and Sunset in Kanyakumari: This is the most popular tourist spot in India from where both sunrise and sunset can be seen. The time of sunrise is around 6 to 6.30 a.m. and that of the sunset is around 6 to 6.30 p.m. though these timings are subject to some variations depending on the time of the year. However, from April to October sunset cannot be seen from here. Moonrise and set also can be seen. The sunset and the moonrise on full moon day is an experience that lives in one's memory for life. On such occasions, one can see the full-fledged golden disc of the moon emerging from the eastern sea, when the sun plunges into the western sea. This is an exhilarating scene to watch.

2. Triveni Sangamam: Triveni Sangamam is another very important tourist spot at the Cape. Tourists both national and international, visit this place to see, how the Bay of Bengal, the Arabian Sea and the Indian Ocean meet. Further, this place is noted for its multicoloured sand, noted for its chemical historical composition and significance.

Sothavilai Beach

This beach is 12 kms from Nagercoil and 12 kms from Kanyakumari on the West Coast Road. It lies in Puthalam Town Panchayat and constitutes one of the best natural beaches of the district. Soft waves of shallow water with lovely sand dunes attract hundreds of domestic tourists here. It is an ideal, idyllic place for holiday lovers in the tropics. The district administration has provided the necessary basic infrastructure facilities like drinking water, shadow shelters, view tower, children's play tools and toilet facilities here.

Sanguthurai Beach

It is a beautiful beach, which is very easily accessible to the local population of Nagercoil. The beach lies in Rajakkamangalam Panchayat Union. It is 13 kms from Nagercoil and 15 kms from Kanyakumari on the West Coast road. There is convenient bus service to this spot from Nagercoil. The district administration has also provided basic infrastructure for tourists here.

Thekkuruchi Beach

Thekkurichi, a tiny village with lovely clam seashore, lies on the west coast road. It is a less known sea shore of Kanyakumari district, lying in the jurisdiction of Rajakkamangalam Panchayat Union. It is a calm seashore village, surrounded by shady thickets of casuarinas creating a spell-binding atmosphere. It is a fine picnic spot and a tourist centre. Coir making is a major small-scale business of the villagers here. This village is situated at a distance of 10 kms from Nagercoil and 29 kms on the West Coast road from Kanyakumari.

Muttom Beach

Located at 16 kms from Nagercoil and 32 kms from Kanyakumari, Muttom is a delightful place on the coast of

Kalkulam, taluk, attracting people desirous of a seaside holiday. The seashore here looks majestic because of the mammoth rocks jutting out right into the sea. The waves dashing against the rocks and falling in huge cascades of water crystals create a mystic atmosphere. Muttom is also a renowned shooting location for both Tamil and Malayalam movies.

This seashore has a rich heritage on account of its ancient lighthouse, originally erected by the British in 1875 and subsequently improved in 1909. The sunset view point here is one of the most enthralling ones in the world. The district administration has developed basic infrastructure facilities like shady shelters, benches, car parking, solar lighting and risk-free fencing on the rocks here.

Thengapattinam Beach

Thengapattinam situated on the West Coast near Painkulam village, in Vilavancode taluk has a fine beach adorned with coconut groves. As coconuts are abundant in this place, the place owes its name Thengapattinam to the coconuts growing in abundances here as coconut is known as 'Thengai' in Tamil. In ancient times this village had direct trade relations with foreign countries like Arabia. There was a busy direct cargo boat service between Thengapattinam and foreign maritime towns. Copra, dry fish, coir and shark fin were the main products that were exported from here.

Thengapattinam has also the estuary of the lovely river Tamiraparani aiming with its non-salty water from the inlands. The back waters in the place are surrounded by breath-taking dense coconut groves. Boat rides on the river backwaters, is really a very pleasant experience. It is 35 kms from Nagercoil and 54 kms from Kanyakumari.

Other Tourist Attractions

The other important tourist attractions in kanyakumari district are Light house in Kanyakumari, Bay-watch, Kids Park, Thiruparappu water falls, Mathoor Thootti Palam and Petchiparai Dam.

Light House in Kanyakumari

From the top of the lighthouse in Kanyakumari at a height of 125 feet, one gets a bird's eye view of Kanyakumari, which is surroundesssd by the sea on three sides and green coconut groves with the tail end of the Western Ghats jutting out on the northern side.

Bay-Watch

It is a water theme amusement park, located at a distance of 2 km on Kanyakumari- Kovalam Road. It is very near to the bus stand. This park has been promoted by Sree Bhadra Parks and Resorts Ltd.,. Thrissur, Kerala.Crazy Chairs, Flying Elephants, Hot tea cups, Cape train, Multiple splash, Milky way, Crazy Cruise, Aqua shuttle, Family Pool, Wave Pool, Sky train etc., constitute some of the main tourist attractions here.

Kids Park

It is located at a distance of 1 km from Kanyakumari near the new bus stand on Kovalam road. Aquarium, Dashing Car, Video games, Skill games, Caterpillar, Columbus ship, Baby train, Aqua dance, Swimming pool, inflatable balloon, Swing Zigzag etc., are all spots which attract tourists to the place.

Thiruparappu Water Falls

Thiruparappu means a pavilion of beauty and sacredness. The panoramic view of Lord Mahadevar temple (Lord Siva) built at a site with green hills and the perennial river Kodayar running in front, presents fascinating and attractive scenary from the shrine. The Kodayar takes a descent at Thiraparappu and the sparkling waterfall makes a rich feast to the eyes of visitors. A Children's Swimming Pool has also been recently constructed here.

Mathoor Thottipalam

The Mathoor trough is the tallest as well as the longest bridge in Asia, built at an altitude of 115 feet. Constructed in 1969, this bridge has become a place of tourist attraction. The bridge has been constructed at Mathoor across the river Parazhiyar and the trough canal on the bridge carries water for irrigation from one side of a hill to the other side. The trough is 384 meters long, with walls having 7 feet height, and 7 feet 6 inches width. The canal is being shouldered by 29 huge pillars. The district administration has created adequate infrastructure facilities for tourists coming over here. It is 60 kms from Kanyakumari.

Petchiparai Dam

It is nearly 62 kms from Kanyakumari and 43 kms from Nagercoil. This dam was built during the days of the Maharaja Sri Moolam Thirunal across the river Kodayar. The dam is 425.1 m long, with a catchment area of 204.8 sq.km. The location of the dam is quite pleasant. It is a fine centre for tourists and can boast of a pleasure boat service too. The dam is surrounded by dense forests with valuable trees, wildlife etc.

Thus, it can be seen that Kanyakumari district abounds with tourist places of scenic splendor, historic heritage and environmental significance. Kanyakumari district, located at the very tip of the land's end of the Indian Peninsula, has a tremendous tourist potential. The entire place can look forward to the arrival of an enormous traffic of tourists both national and international, in the years to come.

REFERENCES

1. *In and around Kanyakumari Tourist Guide Book*, Published by District Collector, Kanyakumari District, Nagercoil, Co-ordination – Tourist Officer, Kanyakumari, July 2003, pp.2-21.
2. Chithambara Krishna R., *Kanyakumari Darsan*, Kanniyakumari Chamus Publications, 1980, p.6.
3. Tamil Nadu Tourism Development Corporation, *The Lands End*, Madras, May 1982.
4. Padmanabhan S., *In and Around Kanyakumari*, Kumar Pathippagam, Nagercoil, p.34.
5. Tamil Nadu Tourism Development Corporation, Kanyakumari, The Land End, Madras, May1982.
6. '*In and Around Kanyakumari Tourist Guide Book*', Published by District Collector, Kanyakumari District, Nagercoil, Co-ordination Tourist Officer, Kanyakumari.
7. *Padmanabhapuram Palace – An Authentic Tourist Guide*, Sree Krishna Nursing Home, Padmanabhapuram, 1997, pp.1-31.

CHAPTER

4

Trends in Tourist Arrival and Hotel Accommodation

Introduction

In this chapter, an attempt has been made to examine the seasonal and irregular variations and the secular trend in tourist arrival in Kanyakumari. The time series analysis would give an idea as to how, more tourists can be attracted by eliminating the lean period and making tourism a round-the-year phenomenon. Further, it analyses the demand and supply of hotel accommodation in Kanyakumari.

The Analytical Framework

In order to study the tourist arrivals over time, a multiplicative model[1] of the following type has been used.

$$Y_t\ (A/P) = T.S.C.I.$$

where

Y_t (A/P) – denotes the time series data on arrivals.

T – denotes the trend component

S – denotes the seasonal variation

C – denotes cyclical movements and

I – denotes the irregular variation.

In order to analyse the trend, the data on tourist arrival were subjected to 12 months' moving average, so as to remove seasonal effect from the time series. Further, to test the significance of the trend over time, the following linear regression equation has been fitted.

$$Y = a + bt \qquad ...(4.1)$$

where,

Y – indicates the tourist arrival

t – indicates time (years)

Exponential growth rates were worked out by using the following formula

$$Y = abt \qquad ...(4.2)$$

where

Y – indicates the arrival

t – indicates time (years)

Compound growth rate is (Antilog b-1) x 100

Irregular variations are computed with the help of the residual method.

$$C = TC/T \qquad ...(4.3)$$

$$I = SI/S \qquad ....(4.4)$$

In order to measure the variability due to trend, seasonal and regular fluctuations, co-efficient of variations are worked out separately for tourist arrival in Kanyakumari.

Trends in Tourist Arrival

Trends in the arrival of domestic and foreign tourists in Kanyakumari and Tamil Nadu during the years 1999-2000 to 2008 – 2009 and monthwise tourist arrivals in Kanyakumari during the years1999-2000 to 2008-2009 are given below.

Domestic and foreign tourist arrival in Tamil Nadu and Kanyakumari from 1999-2000 to 2008-09

Domestic and foreign tourist arrival in Tamil Nadu and Kanyakumari from 1999-2000 to 2008-09 are given in table 4.1.

Table 4.1 shows the tourist arrival in Tamil Nadu from the year 1999-2000 to 2008-2009. Majority i.e., 20.50 percent of the tourists arrived during the year 2008-2009, 16.46 percent during the year 2007-2008 and 13.34 percent during 2006-2007

Table 4.1: Domestic and foreign tourist arrivals in Kanyakumari and Tamil Nadu

Year	Tamil Nadu*				Kanyakumari			
	No. of Domestic Tourists	No of Foreign Tourists	Total	Percentage	No. of Domestic Tourists	No of Foreign Tourists	Total	Percentage
1999-00	18436900	515755	18952655	4.83	1546070	6815	1552885	9.20
2000-01	20010950	692900	20703850	5.27	1778426	8795	1787221	10.60
2001-02	21015875	765320	21781195	5.54	1524277	10655	1534932	9.09
2002-03	27735620	810440	28546060	7.27	1422790	6185	1428975	8.46
2003-04	30241200	981200	31222400	7.95	1506974	7843	1514817	8.97
2004-05	32339000	1179100	33518100	8.52	981497	21353	1002850	5.94
2005-06	39215200	1336118	40551318	10.32	1507988	40914	1548902	9.17
2006-07	50647500	1753255	52400755	13.34	1956873	33481	1990354	11.79
2007-08	62618150	2040300	64658450	16.46	2160272	38912	2199184	13.02
2008-09	78038300	2369220	80407520	20.50	2279243	44267	2323510	13.76

Source: Tourist Information Centre, Kanyakumari, 2010.
*The Hindu, February 16, 2011.

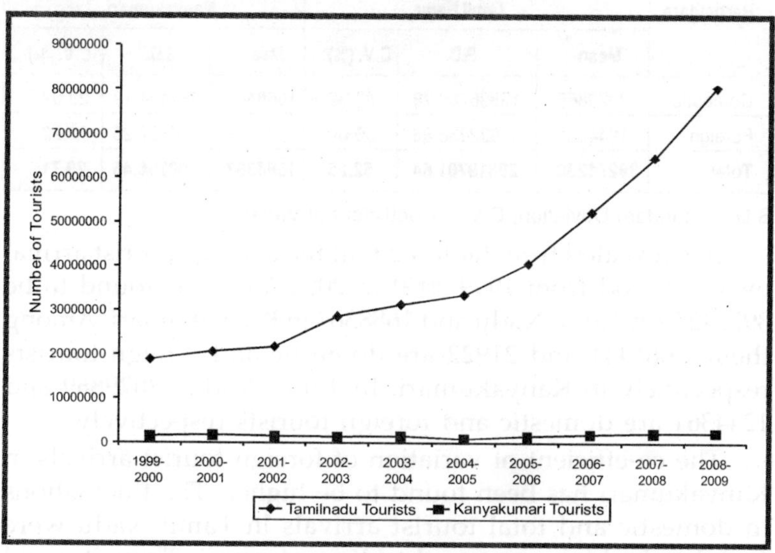

Fig. 4.1. Total tourist arrival in Tamil Nadu and Kanyakumari from 1999-2000 to 2008-2009

and the lowest percent of 4.83 tourists arrived during 1999-2000. In India, Tamil Nadu state is ranks first in domestic and foreign tourist arrival.

Among the domestic and foreign tourist arrivals in Kanyakumari, majority i.e., 13.76 percent have arrived during the year 2008-2009. 13.02 percent during the year 2007-2008, 11.79 percent during the year 2006-2007 and 10.60 percent tourists during 2000-2001. The lowest request of 5.94 percent tourists have arrived during the year 2004-2005. The tourist arrival in Kanyakumari shows a relatively stable trend of growth over the period of study.

The average tourist arrivals in Tamil Nadu and Kanyakumari

The average and the standard deviation pertaining to tourist arrivals in Tamil Nadu and Kanyakumari are presented in table 4.2.

Table 4.2: The average domestic and foreign tourist arrivals and its in stability found in Tamil Nadu and Kanyakumari

Particulars	Tamil Nadu			Kanyakumari		
	Mean	S.D.	C.V. (%)	Mean	S.D.	C.V. (%)
Domestic	38029869	19896762.78	52.32	1666441	384424.19	23.07
Foreign	1244361	622938.86	50.06	21922	15832.26	72.22
Total	**39274230**	**20519701.64**	**52.25**	**1688363**	**400256.45**	**23.71**

S.D. – Standard Deviation, C.V. – Coefficient of Variation.

It is revealed from table 4.2 that the average tourist arrival over a period from 1999-2000 to 2008-2009 was found to be 39274230 in Tamil Nadu and 1688363 in Kanyakumari. Among them, 1666441 and 21922 are domestic and foreign tourists respectively in Kanyakumari. In Tamil Nadu 38029869 and 1244361 are domestic and foreign tourists respectively.

The co-efficient of variation of foreign tourist arrivals in Kanyakumari has been found to be higher. The fluctuations in domestic and total tourist arrivals in Tamil Nadu were found to be high compared to Kanyakumari. Thus, it could be concluded from the analysis that the domestic and total tourists arrivals are more stable over a period of study compared to foreign tourist arrivals.

Month-wise tourist arrival in Kanyakumari

Month-wise tourist arrival in Kanyakumari is given in table 4.3.

It is clear from table 4.3 that the highest percent of 13.80 domestic and foreign tourists arrived in Kanyakumari in month of January. 12.15 percent tourists arrived in the month of May and 11.50 in the month of December. The lowest 4.82 percent of tourists arrival was in the month of July.

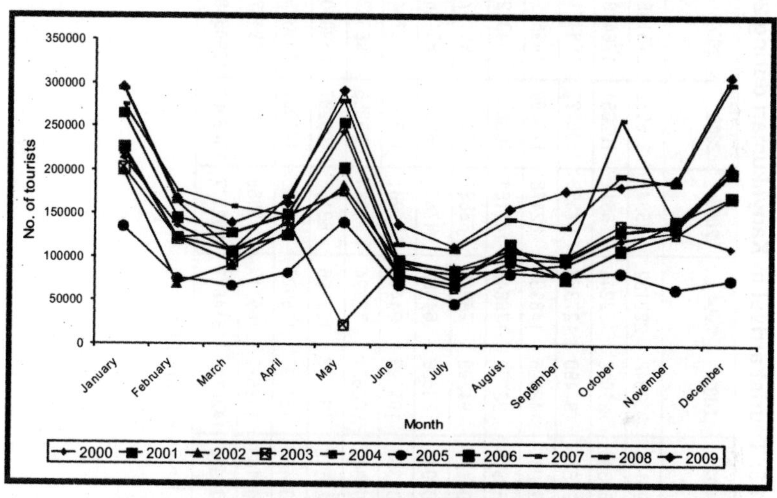

Fig. 4.2. Month-wise tourist arrival in Kanyakumari from during 2000-2009

Seasonal Variations

Seasonal variations in climate make significant impact on tourism. It is a known fact that tourism has been recognized as a seasonal industry. Seasonal variations of tourism in Kanyakumari have been studied by using monthly data on the arrival of domestic and foreign tourists. In order to examine seasonal variations and irregular fluctuations and long term trend in tourist arrival in Kanyakumari, a multiplicative model was used.

Table 4.3: Tourist arrival in Kanyakumari during 2000-2009

Month	2000	2001	2002	2003	2004	2005	2006	2007	2008	2009	Total	Percentage
January	214044	265045	199108	202948	222132	135349	226962	275145	294145	295575	2330453	13.80
February	136611	145478	69398	121012	122245	75511	122651	176478	163485	167665	1300534	7.70
March	107188	128471	90577	94480	127353	67353	106727	158471	107395	139605	1127620	6.68
April	139562	149581	130081	142825	148332	82478	125498	149582	169787	162715	1400441	8.29
May	244311	254302	182819	22770	175648	141183	203633	254312	279955	291965	2050898	12.15
June	89177	97167	94179	94208	78910	68887	80331	96167	115364	138855	953245	5.65
July	81536	85436	86946	73536	64452	47652	69249	85436	107730	112275	814248	4.82
August	85976	98793	108353	105893	94418	81961	115759	98794	144713	156325	1090985	6.46
September	91622	96677	98342	100621	76894	79384	75256	96687	135200	177420	1028103	6.09
October	119888	129766	130512	137777	107796	83156	109267	259000	195080	182420	1454428	8.61
November	131328	137378	138454	134193	126920	64295	142907	141379	185770	190165	1392789	8.25
December	111642	199127	206163	198527	169717	75368	170662	199137	300560	308530	1939433	11.50
Total	**1552885**	**1787221**	**1534932**	**1428790**	**1514817**	**1002577**	**1548902**	**1990588**	**2199184**	**2323515**		

Source: Tourist Information Centre, Kanyakumari, 2010

Seasonal variation is a periodic movement of the variable studied which occurs within a year and it repeats itself year after year due to regular periodic changes in the underlying factors, influencing the variables. In the present study, seasonal variations in the tourist arrival for 10 years have been by applying the moving average method. The details of seasonal indices of arrival of tourists are given in table 4.4.

Table 4.4: Seasonal indices of arrival of domestic and foreign tourists in Kanyakumari from 2000-2009

Month	Seasonal Indices of	
	Domestic Tourists	Foreign Tourists
January	166.16	132.50
February	92.01	119.50
March	80.00	89.37
April	99.66	91.76
May	146.57	95.36
June	67.47	85.19
July	57.60	75.15
August	77.45	82.96
September	72.82	89.34
October	103.47	96.86
November	98.72	116.05
December	138.04	125.95

Source: Tourist Information Centre, Kanyakumari, 2010.

The seasonal changes in the arrival of tourists are mainly caused by the climatic conditions. The analysis has revealed that the period from January to March marks a lean period of arrival of domestic tourists in Kanyakumari. The peak season for tourist arrival is found to be from August to December. The climate during this period is quite conducive for tourists.

In the case of foreign tourist arrival in Kanyakumari is found to be ranging from 75.15 percent to 132.50 percent. During the peak period of August to December, the variations in the seasonal indices of arrival ranges from 82.96 percent to

125.95 percent. Similarly, during the lean period of arrival, the seasonal indices vary from 75.15 percent in July to 91.76 percent in April in the study area.

The seasonal indices of domestic tourist arrival in Kanyakumari is found to be ranging from 57.60 percent to 166.16 percent. During the peak period of August to December, the variations in the seasonal indices of arrival ranges from 77.45 percent to 138.04 percent. Similarly, during the lean period of arrival, the seasonal indices very from 57.60 percent in July to 99.66 percent in April in the study area. The seasonal indices of arrival of domestic and foreign tourists shown in table 4.4 is depicted in Figure 4.3.

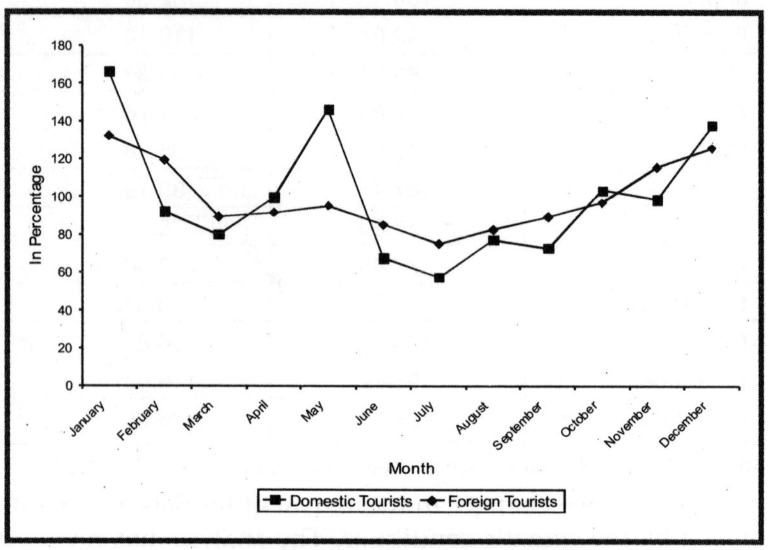

Fig. 4.3. Seasonal indices of arrivals of domestic and foreign tourists in Kanyakumari

Irregular Variations

Irregular variations in the arrival of tourists have been attributed to random factors such as festivals, government functions and the like. The computed data on irregular indices of tourist arrival during the period 2000-2009 are presented in table 4.5.

Table 4.5: Irregular indices of arrival of domestic and foreign tourists in Kanyakumari from 2000-2009

Month	Irregular Indices of	
	Domestic Tourists	Foreign Tourists
January	95.32	99.21
February	96.30	98.61
March	95.14	101.65
April	103.64	112.24
May	113.31	110.21
June	102.11	107.41
July	99.24	100.26
August	95.15	99.81
September	101.60	99.49
October	105.16	101.21
November	109.24	111.45
December	112.32	113.26

Source: Tourist Information Centre, Kanyakumari, 2010.

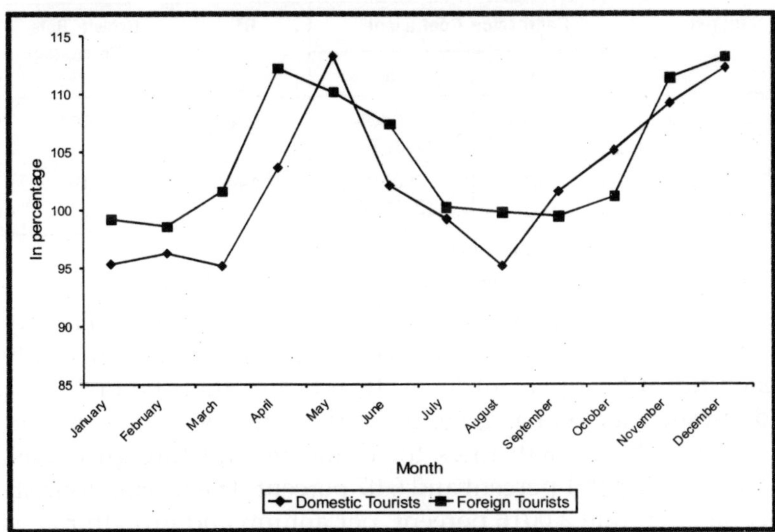

Fig. 4.4. Irregular indices of arrival of domestic and foreign tourists in Kanyakumari from 2000-2009

It is observed from table 4.5 that the irregular indices of domestic tourist arrival varied from 95.14 percent in March to 113.31 percent in May. Similarly, the irregular fluctuations with respect to foreign tourist arrival ranged from 98.61 percent in February to 113.26 percent in December. It can be found from the analysis that the irregular fluctuations in the arrival of domestic tourists were greater than those of foreign tourists over a period of time. This may be due to the fact that social ceremonies and religious festivals cause wide irregular fluctuations in domestic tourist arrival in Kanyakumari. The irregular indices of arrival of domestic and foreign tourists shown in table 4.5 is depicted in Figure 4.4.

Secular Trend and Growth Rate

In order to understand the secular trend of domestic and foreign tourist arrival, equations (4.1) and (4.2) on page 118 have been worked out. The computed results are presented in table 4.6.

Table 4.6: Secular trend and growth rate of arrival of domestic and foreign tourists in kanyakumari

Tourist	Regression Coefficient		R^2	Growth Rate in Percentage
	a	b		
Domestic	14.16	0.040* (2.3679)	0.5286	4.091
Foreign	10.14	0.058* (2.0016)	0.4448	6.07

Figures in brackets are the t-values.

*Indicates that the coefficients are significant at 5 percent level.

The results shown in table 4.6 indicate that the trend co-efficient of domestic tourist arrival is positive and statistically significant at 5 percent level. It indicates that the arrival of domestic tourists has gone up at the rate 2.3679 percent, per annum. The growth rates for domestic and foreign tourist arrivals are 4.091 percent and 6.07 percent. The foreign tourists gone up at rate 2.0016 percent, per annum and growth rate is 6.07 percent. But the trend co-efficient of foreign tourist arrival is statistically significant. It shows that foreign tourist arrival in Kanyakumari is not very significant during the period of study.

Thus, it may be concluded from the time series analysis that the growth trend with regard to tourist arrivals has been more miserable in Kanyakumari than elsewhere in the state. Lean period in the arrival of domestic tourists was observed during the months from January to March. In the case of foreign tourists, lean period is from April to June. The irregular variations have been found to be more among domestic tourist arrivals. A significant positive trend has been observed in the case of domestic tourist arrival in Kanyakumari.

Demand and Supply of Hotel Accommodation

The hotel industry constitutes a very important sector of the tourist infrastructure and is considered to be the king pin of the tourism industry. Among the numerous types of facilities sought by the tourists, accommodation is the foremost item. It is rightly said that "the accommodation facilities" means the places where tourists stop (cease to be travelers) and become guests. The level of guest satisfaction achieved in an area, with regard to its accommodation facilities will, in a large measure, determine the total success of any tourism development programme. Hence, in this section, an attempt has been made to study the trends in the development of boarding and lodging and to examine the demand and supply for accommodation in Kanyakumari.

Trend and Compound growth

The trend about the growth of different types of hotels in the study area has been estimated by using equation 4.2 and the results are given in table 4.7.

Table 4.7 shows that the trend co-efficients are statistically significant at 5 percent level. The value of trend co-efficient is higher for second class hotels when compared to first class, third class and low class hotels. The trend values for first, second, third and low class hotels are 0.08, 0.09, 0.03 and

0.04. Regarding the growth rate of boarding and lodging units in Kanyakumari during the period from 2003 to 2009, the growth rate is higher among the second class hotels, followed by first class, low class and third class hotels respectively. The growth rates are 9.34, 9.98, 3.24 and 4.62 for first, second, third and Low class hotels respectively.

Table 4.7: Trend and compound growth rate estimates of boarding and lodging units (2003-2009)

Sl.No.	Tourist	Trend Coefficient		R^2	Growth Rate Percentage
		a	b		
1.	First Class	2.7987	0.0893* (16.8382)	0.9827	9.34
2.	Second Class	3.0004	0.0951* (7.6100)	0.9205	9.98
3.	Third Class	4.8660	0.0319* (4.3307)	0.7895	3.24
4.	Low Class	5.1176	0.0451* (8.1196)	0.9295	4.62

Figures in brackets are the t-values.

*Indicates that the coefficients are significant at 5 percent level.

Classification and availability of hotel accommodation in the year 2009

The following table 4.8 shows the classification and availability of hotel accommodation in 50 hotels in Kanyakumari in the year 2009. The researcher selected all the fifty hotels as samples. These fifty hotels are classified into four categories namely first class or luxury class, second class or medium class, third class or economy class and low class or very economic class.

In order to find out the total bed capacity available per day in all the four classes of hotels, the number of beds in all the hotels were found out and are given in table 4.8. The tariff rates, as found in the table, represents the rates which prevail during the study period. It is observed from the table that the total number of rooms available during the study period is 1870 with 4812 beds. Out of 1870 rooms, 1344 (71.87 percent) are double bedded and the remaining 526 (28.13 percent) rooms are three to five bedded. The tariff rates vary from less than Rs.500 for low class hotels, Rs.500 to Rs.1500 for economy class, Rs.1500 to Rs.3000 for second class hotels and Rs.3000 to Rs.5000 for first class or luxury class hotels.

Table 4.8: Classification and availability of hotel accommodation in Kanyakumari during the year 2009

Sl. No.	Classification	Tariff Rates (in Rs.)	No. of Hotels	No. of Double Rooms (2 beds)	No. of Family Rooms (3,4,5 beds)	Total No. of Rooms	Total No. of Beds
1.	First Class (Luxury Class)	Rs.3000-5000	16	104	92	196	596
2.	Second Class (Medium Class)	Rs.1500-3000	18	680	296	976	2544
3.	Third Class (Economy Class)	Rs.500-1500	10	466	83	549	1264
4.	Fourth Class (Low Class)	Rs.500 and below	6	94	55	149	408
	Total		50	1344	526	1870	4812

Source: Computed on the Basis of Information of the Tourists Information Centre, Kanyakumari.

Number of beds available in the hotels of Kanyakumari during 2003-2009

Table 4.9 clearly depicts the total number of beds available in the hotels of Kanyakumari during the year 2003 to 2009. Only fifty hotels have been selected by the researcher for the study.

Table 4.9 presents the total bed capacity of all the four classes of hotels in Kanyakumari during the period from 2003 to 2009. The highest bed capacity of 4812 beds was found in the year 2009. 4605 beds in the year 2008 and 4419 beds in the year 2007. The lowest bed capacity of 3393 beds is found in the year 2003. The beds available in Kanyakumari has been steadily increasing year by year.

Table 4.9: Number of beds available in the hotels of Kanyakumari during 2003-2009

Sl.No.	Year	First Class	Second Class	Third Class	Fourth Class	Total Bed Capacity
1.	2003	358	1990	820	225	3393
2.	2004	375	2006	836	250	3467
3.	2005	410	2330	915	284	3939
4.	2006	495	2400	1018	309	4222
5.	2007	525	2480	1018	396	4419
6.	2008	567	2510	1120	408	4605
7.	2009	596	2544	1264	408	4812

Source: Tourist Information Centre, Kanyakumari, 2010.

Demand and supply of beds in the hotels of Kanyakumari

The demand and supply of beds in the hotels of Kanyakumari is given in table 4.10.

Table 4.10: A comparison of demand and supply of hotel accommodation in Kanyakumari during 2003-2009

Sl. No.	Year	Demand for Beds	Supply of Beds (Rate for letting 120 days)	Excess Demand for beds
1.	2003	4072	3393	679
2.	2004	4161	3439	694
3.	2005	4727	3939	788
4.	2006	5067	4222	844
5.	2007	5302	4419	883
6.	2008	5756	4605	1151
7.	2009	6015	4812	1203

Source: Tourist Information Centre, Kanyakumari, 2010.

Note: Beds are let out 120 times in 360 days since the tourists have an average stay of three days.

The number of tourists seeking hotel accommodation (Demand) and the availability of hotel accommodation

(Supply) during the study period are given in table 4.10. Before launching out to study the demand and supply of beds for both domestic and foreign tourists, it becomes imperative for the researcher to assume that all foreign tourists except just a few tourists, prefer first class accommodation. Moreover, those foreign tourists who generally prepare their tour programmes well in advance, book their hotel accommodation also well in advance. Hence, it is natural that first class hotels are booked by such tourists well in advance. However, as it could be seen from Table 4.10, demand for beds is less than the supply of beds during the period of study in Kanyakumari. It indicates that there is demand of beds is in excess of the supply and the excess demand varies from 679 in 2003 to 1203 in 2009.

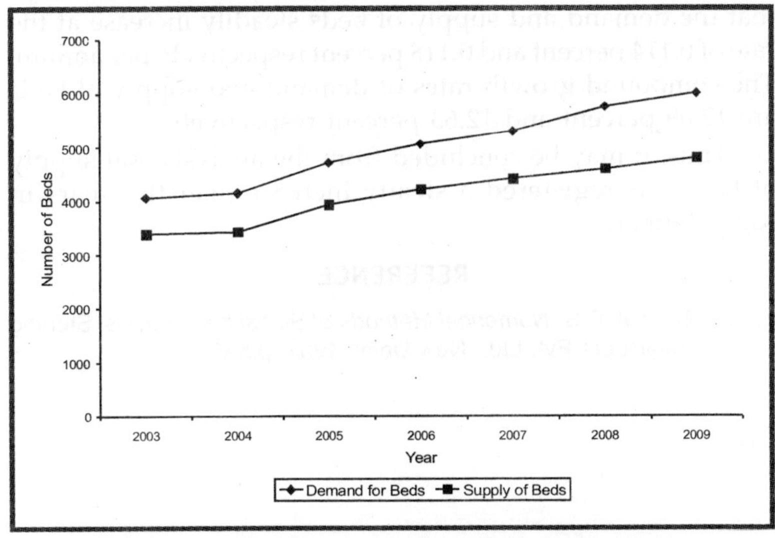

Fig. 4.5. A comparison of demand and supply of hotel accommodation in Kanyakumari during 2003-2009

Trend and growth of demand and supply of beds during 2003 to 2009

In order to find out the trend and growth of the demand and supply of beds, the equation 4.2 was fitted. The estimated results are given in Table 4.11.

Table 4.11: Trend and growth of demand and supply of beds during 2003-2009

Particulars	Trend Coefficient		R^2	Growth Rate in Percentage
	a	b		
Demand	3.9154	0.1141* (12.9417)	0.9710	12.09
Supply	9.0684	0.1188* (15.1367)	0.9786	12.63

Figures in brackets are the t-values.
*Indicates that the coefficients are significant at 5 percent level.

It could be understood from table 4.11 that the trend co-efficients of demand for and supply of beds are statistically significant at 5 percent level and they are positive. It indicates that the demand and supply of beds steadily increase at the rate of 0.114 percent and 0.118 percent respectively per annum. The compound growth rates of demand and supply of beds are 12.09 percent and 12.63 percent respectively.

Thus, it may be concluded from the analysis that supply of beds has registered a steady increase over the years in Kanyakumari.

REFERENCE

1. Grewal, P.S. *Numerical Methods of Statistical Analysis*, Sterling Publishers Pvt. Ltd., New Delhi, 1987, p.555.

CHAPTER 5

Profile of the Tourists, Expenditure Portfolio and its Determinants

Introduction

In this chapter, an attempt has been made to analyse the development of tourism in Kanyakumari from the point of view of the tourists themselves. For this analysis 500 tourists were randomly selected with the help of Tourist Information Centre in Kanyakumari. They were stratified into two strata, namely, domestic and foreign tourists. The first stratum covers 348 samples. The remaining 152 samples come under the second stratum. The data colleted from the selected tourists have been analysed and studied under the following heads:

(*i*) Profile of the tourists

(*ii*) Hotel accommodation and expenditure portfolio and

(*iii*) Determinants of expenditure portfolio

Profile of the Tourists

This section attempts to describe the profile of selected tourists in Kanyakumari.

Nationality of the tourists

The following table 5.1 gives the nationality of the tourists.

The above table shows that 69.60 percentage of the sample tourists are Indians and 30.40 percentage are foreign tourists.

Table 5.1: Nationality of the tourists

Sl. No.	Nationality	No.of Tourists	Percentage
1.	Indian	348	69.60
2.	Foreign	152	30.40
	Total	**500**	**100**

Source: Primary data.

Tourist arrivals from foreign countries

A country-wise distribution of the sample tourists is contained in table 5.2.

Table 5.2: Tourist arrivals from foreign countries and their average duration of stay in Kanyakumari

Sl. No.	Country	No. of Foreign Tourist Arrivals	Percentage to Total	Average Duration of Stay (days)
1.	The United Kingdom	10	6.58	5
2.	Canada	10	6.58	5
3.	Germany	24	15.79	6
4.	France	20	13.16	4
5.	Malaysia	28	18.42	11
6.	Sri Lanka	22	14.47	12
7.	Other countries	38	25.00	8
	Total	**152**	**100**	**7.28**

Source: Primary data

Table 5.2 shows that the foreign tourists stay continuously for 7.28 days on an average. Tourists from Sri Lanka and Malaysia stay for a maximum of 12 and 11 days respectively.

Age

Age-wise distribution of tourists both domestic and foreign, in Kanyakumari is furnished in table 5.3.

Table 5.3 reveals that 68.39 percent of the domestic tourists are in economically active age group of 25-40 years. 22.41

percent and 9.20 percent come under the age groups of below 25 years and above 40 years respectively.

Table 5.3: Age-wise distribution of tourists both domestic and foreign in Kanyakumari

Sl.No.	Age Group	Domestic Tourists		Foreign Tourists	
		No. of Tourists	Percentage	No. of Tourists	Percentage
1.	Below 25 years	78	22.41	10	6.58
2.	25 – 35 years	150	43.10	74	48.68
3.	35 – 40 years	88	25.29	58	38.16
4.	Above 40 years	32	9.20	10	6.58
	Total	**348**	**100**	**152**	**100**

Source: Primary data.

The age-wise distribution of foreign tourists in Kanyakumari infers that 86.84 percent are in the economically active group of 25-40 years. 6.58 percent come under for though the age groups of below 25 years and above 40 years.

Sex

Sex-wise distribution of tourists in Kanyakumari is presented in table 5.4.

Table 5.4: Sex-wise distribution of tourists both domestic and foreign in Kanyakumari

Sl.No.	Sex	Domestic Tourists		Foreign Tourists	
		No. of Tourists	Percentage	No. of Tourists	Percentage
1.	Male	254	72.99	106	69.74
2.	Female	94	27.01	46	30.26
	Total	**348**	**100**	**152**	**100**

Source: Primary data.

It is clearly understood from table 5.4 that domestic tourists group is dominated by male tourists. In Kanyakumari, the male tourists have outnumbered female tourists by 27 percent.

Similar results were also observed in the case of foreign tourists. The sex-wise distribution of foreign tourists shows that male tourists dominate in Kanyakumari. The survey further revealed that the male tourists outnumbered female tourists by 30 percent.

Marital status

The marital status of the sample tourists is presented in table 5.5.

Table 5.5: Marital status of tourists both domestic and foreign in Kanyakumari

Sl.No.	Marital Status	Domestic Tourists		Foreign Tourists	
		No. of Tourists	Percentage	No. of Tourists	Percentage
1.	Married	262	75.29	98	64.47
2.	Unmarried	86	24.71	54	35.53
	Total	**348**	**100**	**152**	**100**

Source: Primary data.

It is clearly revealed from table 5.5 that majority of the domestic tourists are married constituting 75.29 percent and 24.71 percent are unmarried. Among foreign tourists 64.47 percent are married and 35.53 percent are unmarried.

Educational level

The following table 5.6 shows the educational level of the tourists.

Table 5.6: Educational level of the tourists

Sl.No.	Educational Level	Domestic Tourists		Foreign Tourists	
		No. of Tourists	Percentage	No. of Tourists	Percentage
1	School Level	20	5.74	2	1.32
2	Graduate	193	55.46	30	19.74
3	Post Graduate	75	21.55	68	44.74
4	Professional	60	17.25	52	34.20
	Total	**348**	**100**	**152**	**100**

Source: Primary data

Table 5.6 shows that 20 (5.74 percent) domestic tourists have school level education. 193 (55.46 percent) tourists are graduates, 75 (21.55 percent) are post graduates and 60 (17.25 percent) tourists are professional degree holders.

In the case of foreign tourists 2 (1.32 percent) tourists have school level education, 30 (19.74 percent) tourists are graduates, 68 (44.74 percent) tourists are post graduates and 52 (34.20 percent) are professional degree holders.

Occupation-wise distribution of tourists

Occupation-wise distribution of tourists who visit Kanyakumari is presented in table 5.7.

Table 5.7: Occupation-wise distribution of tourists visiting Kanyakumari

Sl.No.	Occupation	Domestic Tourists		Foreign Tourists	
		No. of Tourists	Percentage	No. of Tourists	Percentage
1.	Private Employment	92	26.44	58	38.15
2.	Govt. Employment	56	16.09	13	8.60
3.	Business	82	23.56	26	17.10
4.	Professional	64	18.39	45	29.61
5.	Student	30	8.62	10	6.58
6.	Agriculture	24	6.90	—	—
	Total	**348**	**100**	**152**	**100**

Source: Primary data

It is clearly understood from table 5.7 that out of 348 domestic tourists majority i.e., 92 (26.44 percent) have private employment followed by 82 (23.56 percent) of the sample tourists who are businessmen, 64 (18.39 percent) tourists are professionals, 56 (16.09 percent) have government employment, 30 (8.62 percent) are students and 24 (6.90 percent) tourists are agriculturalists respectively.

The foreign tourists visiting Kanyakumari generally, came from various walks of life. The investigator could see from her survey that 58 (38.15 percent) have private employment, 45 (29.61 percent) tourists are professionals, 26 (17.10 percent) are businessmen, 13 (8.60 percent) tourists have government employment and 10 (6.58 percent) tourists are students. Thus it is evident that tourism is capable of luring people with different occupations.

Monthly income of the Domestic Tourists

The table 5.8 shows the monthly income of the domestic tourists in Kanyakumari.

Table 5.8: Monthly income of the domestic tourists

Sl.No.	Monthly Income	No. of Tourists	Percentage
1.	Below Rs.10,000	42	12.07
2.	Rs.10,000-Rs.25,000	166	47.70
3.	Rs.25,000-Rs.50,000	95	27.30
4.	Above Rs.50,000	45	12.93
	Total	**348**	**100**

Source: Primary data.

Table 5.8 shows that the distribution of tourists based on their monthly income. Out of 348 domestic tourists, 42 (12.07 percent) tourists earn below Rs. 10,000, 166 (47.70 percent) tourists earn

Rs. 10,000 to Rs.25,000, 95 (27.30 percent) tourists earn Rs.25,000 to Rs.50,000 and 45 (12.93 percent) tourists earn above Rs. 50,000.

Monthly income of the foreign tourists

The following table 5.9 shows the distributions of foreign tourists based on their monthly income.

Table 5.9: Monthly income of the foreign tourists

Sl.No.	Monthly Income	No. of Tourists	Percentage
1	Below Rs.50,000	16	10.53
2	Rs.50,000-Rs.75,000	28	18.42
3	Rs.75,000-Rs.1,00,000	75	49.34
4	Above Rs.1,00,000	33	21.71
	Total	**152**	**100**

Source: Primary data.

Table 5.9 reveals the monthly income of the foreign tourists. Out of 152 foreign tourists 16 (10.53 percent) tourists earn below Rs.50,000, 28 (18.42 percent) earn Rs. 50,000 to Rs.75,000, 75 (49.34 percent) earn Rs.75,000 to Rs.1,00,000 and 33 (21.71 percent) tourists earn above Rs.1,00,000.

Factors that influence the tourists to visit Kanyakumari

Table 5.10 explains the factors, which influence the flow of tourists in Kanyakumari.

Table 5.10: Factors that influence the tourists to visit Kanyakumari

Sl.No.	Source	Domestic Tourists		Foreign Tourists	
		No. of Tourists	Percen-tage	No. of Tourists	Percen-tage
1.	Friends	112	32.18	10	6.58
2.	From tour guide Books	22	6.32	68	44.74
3.	Relatives	98	28.16	8	5.26
4.	Non-Indian Tour Operator	-	-	30	19.74
5.	Media	41	11.79	10	6.58
6.	Indian Tour Operator	31	8.91	6	3.95
7.	Tourism Board of India	44	12.64	20	13.16
	Total	**348**	**100**	**152**	**100**

Source: Primary data.

It could be inferred from table 5.10 that domestic tourists who are influenced by friends constitute 32.18 percent followed by those influenced by relatives constituting 28.16 percent.

It is clear from the above table that from tour guide books exercise the maximum influence on foreign tourists. Around 44.74 percent of the foreign tourists came to Kanyakumari, learning from books the salient features of the centres of tourism throughout Kanyakumari in general. Non-Indian tour operators also wield a tremendous share of 19.74 percent.

Frequency of earlier visit

Table 5.11 shows the details of the frequency of earlier visits to Kanyakumari.

Table 5.11: Frequency of earlier visits

Sl.No.	Frequency	No. of Tourists	Percentage
1.	Below 3 Times	9	3.60
2.	3-5 Times	65	26.00
3.	5-7 Times	21	8.40
4.	7-10 Times	16	6.40
5.	10-15 Times	21	8.40
6.	More than 15 Times	118	47.20
	Total	**250**	**100**

Source: Primary data.

Considering the frequency of earlier visits by the 250 both domestic and foreign tourists, it is found that 3.60 percent have visited Kanyakumari below 3 times, 26 percent 3-5 times, 8.40 percent 5-7 times, 6.40 percent 7-10 times, 8.40 percent 10-15 times and the remaining 47.20 percent have visited more than 15 times.

Purpose of Earlier Visit

The following table 5.12 shows the purposes of earlier visits to Kanyakumari.

Table 5.12: Purpose of earlier visit

Sl.No.	Purpose	Domestic Tourists		Foreign Tourists	
		No. of Tourists	Percentage	No. of Tourists	Percentage
1.	Tour Programme	45	25.86	28	36.84
2.	Pleasure	40	22.98	21	27.63
3.	Business	15	8.63	5	6.58
4.	Education	18	10.35	4	5.26
5.	Sports	20	11.49	8	10.53
6.	Health	36	20.69	10	13.16
	Total	**174**	**100**	**76**	**100**

Source: Primary data

Table 5.12 shows the purpose of earlier visit of both domestic and foreign tourists. Out of 174 domestic tourists who have visited Kanyakumari earlier. 45 (25.86 percent) visited for tour purpose, 40 (22.98 percent) visit for pleasure, 15 (8.63 percent) for business, 18 (10.35 percent) visit for education, 20 (11.49 percent) visit for sports and 36 (20.69 percent) for health purpose.

In the case of foreign tourists 28 (36.84 percent) tourists visited for tour purpose, 21 (27.63 percent) for pleasure, 5 (6.58 percent) for business, 4 (5.26 percent) for education, 8 (10.53 percent) for sports and the remaining 10 (13.16 percent) tourists visited for health purpose.

Kanyakumari's position in the Travel Itinerary

Kanyakumari's position in the travel itinerary of both the foreign and Indian visitors could be seen from table 5.13.

Table 5.13: Kanyakumari's position in the travel itinerary

Sl.No.	Position	Domestic Tourists		Foreign Tourists	
		No. of Tourists	Percentage	No. of Tourists	Percentage
1.	First Destination	280	80.46	16	10.52
2.	Extension tour from other parts of India	68	19.54	120	78.96
3.	Extension tour from other countries	—	—	16	10.52
	Total	**348**	**100**	**152**	**100**

Source: Primary data.

Table 5.13 shows the position of Kanyakumari in the travel itinerary of both domestic and foreign tourists. In the case of domestic tourists for 280 (80.46 Percent) tourists it is their first destination, for 68 (19.54 percent) it is an extension tour from other parts of India.

In the case of foreign tourists for 120 (78.96 percent) tourists it is an extension tour from other parts of India, for 16 (10.52 percent) tourists it is their first destination and for 16 (10.52 percent) tourists it is an extension tour from other countries.

Mode of transport to reach Kanyakumari

The mode of transport used by both domestic and foreign tourists to reach Kanyakumari is presented in table 5.14.

Table 5.14: Mode of transport to reach Kanyakumari

Sl.No.	Mode of Transport to Kanyakumari	Domestic Tourists		Foreign Tourists	
		No. of Tourists	Percentage	No. of Tourists	Percentage
1.	Bus	72	20.69	4	2.63
2.	Own Car/Tourist Car	268	77.01	68	44.74
3.	Government Tourist Vehicle	8	2.30	80	52.63
	Total	**348**	**100**	**152**	**100**

Source: Primary data

It is found from table 5.14 that in the case of domestic tourists, road transport is predominant significance. Transport by bus constitutes 20.69 percent, by own car/ tourist car constitute 77.01 percent and by government tourist vehicle constitute 2.30 percent of the domestic tourists.

Further, it is observed that in the case of foreign tourists, government tourist vehicle transport figures to be the most important. In Kanyakumari too, government tourist vehicles occupy the first place with 52.63 percent followed by own car/tourist car with 44.74 percent and by bus constituting 2.63 percent of the tourists.

Opinion about transport availed

The table 5.15 shows that opinion about transport availed by domestic and foreign tourists.

Table 5.15 shows the opinions of both domestic and foreign tourists about the mode of transport availed. It is inferred that 'flight' is ranked first with the weighted average score of 4.33, and it is highly expensive, 'Ship' is ranked second with the weighted average score of 2.76 and it is expensive, 'Taxi' is ranked third with the weighted average score of 2.67 with medium expense, 'Public transport: train' is ranked fourth with the weighted average score of 2.63 with medium expense,

'Tourist bus' is ranked fifth with the weighted average score of 1.95 and 'Public transport : Bus' is ranked last and rated to be cheap.

Table 5.15: Opinion about mode of transport availed

S. No.	Factors	No. of Highly expensive (5)	No. of Expensive (4)	No. of Normal (3)	No. of Cheap (2)	No. of Very Cheap (1)	Total Score	Weig-hted average score	Rank
		No. of Tourists	No. of Tourists	No. of Tourists	No. of Tourists	No. of Tourists			
1.	Flight	295 [1475]	105 [420]	80 [240]	12 [24]	8 [8]	2167	4.33	I
2.	Taxi	55 [275]	61 [244]	85 [255]	265 [530]	34 [34]	1338	2.67	III
3.	Tourist Buses	10 [50]	20 [80]	25 [75]	325 [650]	120 [120]	975	1.95	V
4.	Public Transport: Bus	2 [10]	10 [40]	15 [45]	55 [110]	418 [418]	623	1.25	VI
5.	Public Transport: Train	45 [225]	75 [300]	108 [324]	197 [394]	75 [75]	1318	2.63	IV
6.	Ship	35 [175]	85 [340]	92 [376]	200 [400]	88 [88]	1379	2.76	II

Source: Primary data

Note: Figures in brackets represent weightage

The most delightful tourism activity in Kanyakumari

The following table 5.16 shows that the most delightful tourism activity in Kanyakumari for tourists and Garrett ranking technique has been adopted.

Table 5.16 clearly exhibits the most delightful tourism activity in Kanyakumari for domestic and foreign tourists. In the case of domestic tourists, the most delightful activity is visiting the 'religious places' and is ranked first with the highest mean score of 56.47, 'boating' is ranked second with the mean score of 55.79, 'historical place' is ranked third with the mean score of 53.01, 'sight seeing' is ranked fourth with the mean score of 48.57, 'Amusement park' is ranked fifth with the mean score of 47.22, 'trekking' is ranked sixth with the mean score of 44.63 and 'traditional and cultural values' ranked last with the mean score of 44.29.

Table 5.16: The most delightful tourism activity in Kanyakumari

Sl. No	Factors	Domestic Tourists		Foreign Tourists	
		Mean score	Rank	Mean score	Rank
1.	Boating	55.79	II	57.47	I
2.	Amusement Park	47.22	V	48.84	IV
3.	Religious Places	56.47	I	46.95	VII
4.	Trekking	44.63	VI	50.59	II
5.	Sight seeing	48.57	IV	49.89	III
6.	Historical place	53.01	III	48.38	V
7.	Traditional & Cultural Values	44.29	VII	47.89	VI

Source: Primary data

In the case of foreign tourists the most delightful activity is 'boating' and is ranked first with the highest mean score of 57.47 followed by 'trekking' which is ranked second with the mean score of 50.59, 'sight seeing' ranking third with the mean score of 49.89, 'Amusement park' ranking fourth with the mean score of 48.84, 'historical place' ranking fifth with the mean score of 48.38, 'traditional & cultural values' ranking sixth with the mean score of 47.89 and 'religious places' ranking last with the mean score of 46.95.

Arrangement of the tour

The methods of arrangement of the tour are given in the following table 5.17.

It is found from table 5.17 that in the case of domestic tourists 161 (46.26 percent) arrange the tour through self, 55 (15.80 percent) tourists through institution, 22 (6.32 percent) tourists through travel agents and 110 (31.62 percent) tourists through friends/ relatives respectively.

Further, it is observed that in the case of foreign tourists, 28 (18.42 percent) tourists, arrange the tour by themselves, 30 (19.74 percent) tourists through institution, 90 (59.21

percent) tourists through travel agents and 4 (2.63 percent) tourists through friends/relatives respectively.

Table 5.17: Methods of arrangement of the tour

Sl.No.	Methods of arrangements	Domestic Tourists		Foreign Tourists	
		No. of Tourists	Percentage	No. of Tourists	Percentage
1.	Self	161	46.26	28	18.42
2.	Institution	55	15.80	30	19.74
3.	Travel agents	22	6.32	90	59.21
4.	Friends/Relatives	110	31.62	4	2.63
	Total	**348**	**100**	**152**	**100**

Source: Primary data.

Distribution of tourists on the purpose of their visit to Kanyakumari

Distribution of tourists on the purpose of their visit in Kanyakumari is given in the following table 5.18.

Table 5.18: Distribution of tourists based on the purpose of their visit to Kanyakumari

Sl.No.	Purpose	Domestic Tourists		Foreign Tourists	
		No. of Tourists	Percentage	No. of Tourists	Percentage
1.	Leisure (Sight Seeing)	254	72.99	130	85.53
2.	Health	4	1.15	4	2.63
3.	Religion	6	1.72	—	—
4.	Education	40	11.49	12	7.89
5.	Visiting Friends	8	2.30	—	—
6.	Business	4	1.15	—	—
7.	Others	32	9.20	6	3.95
	Total	**348**	**100**	**152**	**100**

Source: Primary data.

A cursory glance at the above table 5.18 makes it clear that annual programmes of sight-seeing constitutes the major purpose for the tours. The investigator could see from her sample survey that 85.53 percent of the foreign tourists visit Kanyakumari merely for spending their holidays in sight-seeing. This is quite true for both the domestic and foreign tourists. Education and others come next in importance. Thus it is evident that man is generally lured to a place where they can feast their eyes on different kinds of scenic beauty. Kanyakumari enjoys the unique distinction of having been endowed with all these.

Hotel Accommodation and Expenditure Portfolio of Selected Tourists

In this section, an attempt has been made to analyse the hotel accommodation and patterns of expenditure of the sample tourists.

Sources of information about the hotel

Table 5.19 shows the sources of information about the hotels in Kanyakumari.

Table 5.19: Sources of information about the hotels

Sl.No.	Sources	No. of Tourists	Percentage
1.	Travel Agent	210	42.00
2.	Friends	108	21.60
3.	Advertisements	92	18.40
4.	Tour Operators	50	10.00
5.	Tourist guides	40	8.00
	Total	**500**	**100**

Source: Primary data.

It is inferred from table 5.19 that out of 500 tourists, majority i.e., 210 (42 percent) tourists have their source of information about hotels from travel agents followed by friends which constitute 108 (21.60 percent) and 92 (18.40 percent) get such information through advertisements, 50 (10 percent) and 40 (8 percent) of the tourists got from tour operator and tourist guides respectively.

Mode of transport used to reach the hotel

Table 5.20 gives the various modes of transport availed by the tourists to reach the hotel.

Table 5.20: Mode of transport used to reach the hotel

Sl.No.	Mode of transport	No. of Tourists	Percentage
1.	Taxi	110	22.00
2.	Car	186	37.20
3.	Auto-rickshaw	104	20.80
4.	By walk	70	14.00
5.	Company coach etc.	30	6.00
	Total	**500**	**100**

Source: Primary data.

An analysis of the modes of transport used by the tourists to reach the hotel of their stay reveals that 110 (22 percent) of them use taxi, 186 (37.20 percent) use car, 104 (20.80 percent) use auto-rickshaw, 70 (14 percent) reach the hotel by walk and the remaining 30 (6 percent) use company coach.

Average number of days in India stayed by foreign tourists

The following table 5.21 shows the average number of days in India by stayed foreign tourists.

Table 5.21: Average number of days stayed by foreign tourists in India

Sl.No.	Days	No. of Tourists	Percentage
1.	1-10	14	9.21
2.	10-20	18	11.84
3.	20-30	59	38.82
4.	30-40	47	30.92
5.	40-50	14	9.21
	Total	**152**	**100**

Source: Primary data.

The above table shows the average number of days of stay of foreign tourists in India. Out of the 152 foreign tourists surveyed, 14 (9.21 percent) has stayed in India for less than 10 days, 18 (11.84 percent) stayed for 10-20 days, 59 (38.82 percent) stayed for 20-30 days, 47 (30.92 percent) for 30-40 days and the rest 14 (9.21 percent) stayed in India for 40-50 days.

Actual stay as against the original plan

Actual stay as against original plan of foreign tourists is given in the following table 5.22.

Table 5.22: Actual stay as against the original plan

Sl.No.	Stay	No. of Tourists	Percentage
1.	More than planned	22	14.47
2.	Less than planned	86	56.58
3.	Exactly as planned	44	28.95
	Total	**152**	**100.00**

Source: Primary data.

The study analyses whether the actual stay by the foreign tourists has differed from their original plan of stay in India. In more than 70 percent of the cases, the actual stay has differed from the original plan of stay. 22 (14.47 percent) of the foreign tourists have stayed in India for more than the proposed number of days, 86 (56.58 percent) have stayed in India less than the proposed number of days and 44 (28.95 percent) have stayed in India exactly as planned.

Tourists' preference as to the category of hotels

The following table 5.23 shows the tourists' preference as to the category of hotels.

Table 5.23: Tourists' preference as to the category of hotels

Sl.No.	Categories of Hotel	Domestic tourists	Percen -tage	Foreign tourists	Percen-tage	Total	Percen-tage
1.	3 star	26	7.47	82	53.95	108	21.60
2.	2 star	68	19.54	48	31.58	116	23.20
3.	1 star	80	22.99	12	7.90	92	18.40
4.	Non-star	174	50.00	10	6.58	184	36.80
	Total	**348**	**100**	**152**	**100.00**	**500**	**100**

Source: Primary data.

Though 63.20 percent of the tourists preferred One to Three star hotels for their stay, only 36.80 percent of them are able to get accommodation according to their preference.

However, those tourists who preferred One to Three star hotels but could not get accommodation were forced to select non star hotels for their stay. Another major fact is that the problem of not getting accommodation in the hotels of their preference is mostly pronounced among foreign tourists.

Reasons for selection of one to three star hotels by foreign tourists

Reasons for selecting one to three star hotels by foreign tourists is given in the following table 5.24.

Table 5.24: Reasons for selection of one to three star hotels by foreign tourists

Sl.No.	Reasons	No. of Tourists	Percentage
1.	Cost not commensurating with the benefit	82	57.75
2.	Lack of Technological convenience	52	36.62
3.	Difficulties in advance booking	8	5.63
	Total	**142**	**100**

Source: Primary data.

It is evident from the above table 5.24 that out of the 142 (one to three star preferred) foreign tourists, 82 (57.75 percent) tourists feel that the cost is not commensurating with the benefit, 52 (36.62 percent) tourists feel there is lack of technology and 8 (5.63 percent) tourists face difficulties in advance booking.

Tourists' preference to the plan types

The following table 5.25 shows the tourists preference as to the plan types.

The data concerning tourists' preference as to the plan types are also collected and displayed in the above table. Out of the 500 tourists, 68 percent prefer European plan, 16 percent prefer Modified American plan, 9.20 percent prefer American plan and the remaining 6.80 percent prefer other plans like package plan and off seasonal concession plan.

Table 5.25: Tourists' preference to the plan types

Sl.No.	Plan	No. of Tourists	Percentage
1.	European	340	68.00
2.	American	46	9.20
3.	Modified American	80	16.00
4.	Others	34	6.80
	Total	**500**	**100**

Source: Primary data

Types of rooms preferred by the Tourists

Types of rooms preferred by the tourists are given in the following table 5.26.

Table 5.26: Types of rooms preferred by the tourists

Sl.No.	Type of rooms	No. of Tourists	Percentage
1.	Single	258	19.60
2.	Double	98	51.60
3.	Suites	40	8.00
4.	Other type of rooms	104	20.80
	Total	**500**	**100**

Source: Primary data

Regarding the tourists preference to the types of room, 51.60 percent prefer to stay in double room, 19.60 percent in single room and 8 percent in suites and other types of rooms are preferred by 20.80 percent of the tourists.

Tourists Evaluation of Hotel Facilities and Services

This section attempts to describe the factors influencing the choice of hotels, method of booking hotel rooms, preference to the location of hotels, opinion about the area, food habits, prices charged, taste of food & beverage, and various services and facilities in hotels.

Factors influencing the choice of hotels

There are certain crucial factors acting as guidelines in choosing a hotel of one's choice. Path finders survey held in

1987 revealed that quality of food, room service facility, image of the hotel and room tariff are the most major pointers in the selection of hotels. Health club and swimming pool facilities are no growing factors, but the image has its own advantage.

Selection of a hotel by the tourists for their stay depends upon their final evaluation of hotel services and facilities. It is in fact a process in which many factors interact and these factors must be given due weightage. Hence, a weighted ranking method is used to evaluate the various factors governing the selection of hotels by the tourists.

The factors considered for evaluation include star rating, room service quality, room facility, health club, games court, conference hall, swimming pool, room size, banquettes, quality of food, image of the hotel, workers hospitality, bar and world wide net work reservation.

1. Factors influencing the choice of hotels among domestic tourists: Table 5.27 shows the factors influencing the choice of hotels among domestic tourists.

Table 5.27: Factors influencing hotel choice among domestic tourists

S No.	Factors	No. of Highly expensive (5)	No. of Expensive (4)	No. of Normal (3)	No. of Cheap (2)	No. of Very Cheap (1)	Total Score	Weig-hted average score	Rank
		No. of Tourists	No. of Tourists	No. of Tourists	No. of Tourists	No. of Tourists			
1	2	3	4	5	6	7	8	9	10
1.	Food Quality	95 475	84 336	127 381	21 42	21 21	1255	3.61	IV
2.	Hotel Image	142 710	134 536	42 126	22 44	8 8	1424	4.09	I
3.	Workers' Hospitality	130 650	148 592	40 120	6 12	24 24	1398	4.02	II
4.	Room service quality	110 550	142 568	54 162	34 68	8 8	1356	3.90	III
5.	Room facility	74 370	75 300	74 222	76 152	49 49	1093	3.14	VII

1	2	3	4	5	6	7	8	9	10
6.	Room size	38 [190]	142 [568]	70 [210]	76 [152]	22 [22]	1142	3.28	VI
7.	Star rating	44 [220]	132 [528]	74 [222]	78 [156]	20 [20]	1146	3.29	V
8.	Worldwide net work reservation	58 [290]	78 [312]	64 [192]	90 [180]	58 [58]	1032	2.97	VIII
9.	Conference Hall	22 [110]	62 [248]	94 [282]	140 [280]	30 [30]	950	2.73	IX
10.	Bar	42 [210]	48 [192]	34 [102]	158 [316]	66 [66]	886	2.55	X
11.	Banquet	16 [80]	32 [128]	82 [246]	162 [324]	56 [56]	834	2.40	XI
12.	Swimming Pool	10 [50]	18 [72]	76 [228]	182 [364]	62 [62]	776	2.23	XII
13.	Health Club	4 [20]	26 [104]	52 [156]	186 [372]	80 [80]	732	2.10	XIII
14.	Games Court	14 [70]	26 [104]	42 [126]	98 [196]	168 [168]	664	1.91	XIV

Source: Primary data

Note: Figures in brackets represent weightage

Table 5.27 it is observed that in the case of domestic tourists the factor, 'hotel image' is ranked first with the highest weighted average score of 4.09, 'workers hospitality' is ranked second with the weighted average score of 4.02, 'room service quality' is ranked third with the weighted average score of 3.90, 'food quality' is ranked fourth with the weighted average score of 3.61, 'star rating' is ranked fifth with the weighted average score of 3.29, 'room size' is ranked sixth with the weighted average score of 3.28 and room facility, world wide net work reservation, conference hall, bar, banquet, swimming pool, health club, games court are subsequently ranked by the domestic tourists. The first six are very important and the remaining are considered less important by the domestic tourists.

2. Factors influencing the choice of hotel among foreign tourists: Table 5.28 shows the factors influencing the choice of hotel among foreign tourists.

Table 5.28: Factors influencing hotel choice among foreign tourists

Sl. No.	Factors	No. of Highly expensive (5)		No. of Expensive (4)		No. of Normal (3)		No. of Cheap (2)		No. of Very Cheap (1)		Total Score	Weighted average score	Rank
		No. of Tourists		No. of Tourists		No. of Tourists		No. of Tourists		No. of Tourists				
1.	Food Quality	70	350	52	208	14	42	8	16	8	8	624	3.95	II
2.	Hotel Image	78	390	40	160	22	66	6	12	6	6	634	4.01	I
3.	Workers' Hospitality	56	280	60	240	14	42	10	20	12	12	594	3.76	III
4.	Room service quality	34	170	64	256	18	54	14	28	22	22	530	3.35	V
5.	Room facility	26	130	72	288	26	78	22	44	6	6	546	3.46	IV
6.	Room size	18	90	62	248	30	90	30	60	12	12	500	3.16	VII
7.	Star rating	26	130	46	184	28	84	36	72	16	16	486	3.08	IX
8.	Worldwide net work reservation	32	160	38	152	34	102	42	84	6	6	504	3.19	VI
9.	Conference Hall	10	50	34	136	44	132	58	116	6	6	440	2.78	X
10.	Bar	34	170	38	152	18	54	52	104	10	10	490	3.10	VIII
11.	Banquet	10	50	22	88	28	84	62	124	30	30	376	2.38	XII
12.	Swimming Pool	8	40	12	32	34	102	72	144	26	26	344	2.18	XIII
13.	Health Club	4	20	16	64	42	126	86	172	4	4	386	2.44	XI
14.	Games Court	10	50	14	56	32	96	16	32	80	80	314	1.99	XIV

Source: Primary data.

Note: Figures in brackets represent weightage.

From the table 5.28 it is inferred that in the case of foreign tourists, among all the factors, 'hotel image' is ranked first with the highest weighted average score of 4.01, 'food quality' is ranked second with the weighted average score of 3.95, 'workers hospitality' is ranked third with the weighted average score of 3.76, 'room facility' is ranked fourth with the weighted average score of 3.46, 'room service quality' is ranked fifth with the weighted average score of 3.35, 'world wide net work reservation' is ranked sixth with the weighted average score of 3.19 and room size, bar, star rating, conference hall, health club, banquet, swimming pool and games court have subsequent ranks given by the foreign tourists. The first six are very important and the remaining are considered less important by the foreign tourists.

Method of booking hotel rooms by the tourists

The following table 5.29 shows the method of booking hotel rooms by the tourists.

Table 5.29: Method of booking rooms by the tourists

Sl.No.	Method	No. of Tourists	Percentage
1.	Direct spot booking	264	52.80
2.	Direct advance booking	106	21.20
3.	Advance booking through travel agents	70	14.00
4.	Advance booking through company travel departments, travel club, friends, etc.	60	12.00
	Total	**500**	**100**

Source: Primary data

Table 5.29 reveals that out of 500 tourists, 264 (52.80 percent) tourists are booking rooms through direct spot booking, 106 (21.20 percent) tourists through direct advance booking, 70 (14 percent) through travel agents in advance and 60 (12 percent) tourists through company, travel departments, travel club, friends, etc., in advance.

Tourists' general preference to the location of hotels

The following table 5.30 shows the tourists' general preference as to the location of hotels.

It is obvious from the above table that the tourists' general preference to the location of the hotels, 60.80 percent are in favour of downtown area', 22 percent prefer 'seashore' and 17.20 percent prefer to stay 'near the railway station' to have easy access.

Table 5.30: Tourists' general preference to the location of hotels

Sl.No.	Nature of location	No. of Tourists	Percentage
1.	Downtown area	304	60.80
2.	Near Railway station	86	17.20
3.	Seashore	110	22
	Total	**500**	**100**

Source: Primary data.

Location of hotels preferred by domestic tourists

The evaluation of the location of hotel, usually on the basis of accessibility to downtown area, near railway station and seashore. The ranking method is used to identify the extent of influence of these factors. Six grades are assigned namely 'outstanding' (5 points), 'very good' (4 points), 'good' (3 points), 'average' (2 points), 'poor' (1 point) and 'no comment' (0 point). Table 5.31 shows the location of hotels preferred by domestic tourists.

Table 5.31: Location of hotel preferred domestic tourists

Sl.No.	Grade	Down-town Area	Scores	Near Railway Station	Scores	Seas-hore	Scores
1.	Outstanding (5)	130	650	36	180	78	390
2.	Very good (4)	58	232	132	528	96	384
3.	Good (3)	68	204	116	348	108	324
4.	Average (2)	32	64	42	84	38	76
5.	Poor (1)	30	30	22	22	28	28
6.	No comment(0)	30	0	-	-	-	-
	Total	**348**	**1,180**	**348**	**1,162**	**348**	**1,202**

Source: Primary data.

From the table 5.31 it is inferred that the ranking on the location of hotels reveals that in the case of domestic tourists, the 'Seashore' gets the first rank with 1202 scores followed by 'Downtown area' with 1180 scores and railway station with 1162 scores.

Location of hotel stayed in by foreign tourists

Table 5.32 presents the ranking of the location of hotels stayed in by foreign tourists.

Table 5.32: Location of hotel stayed in by foreign tourists

Sl.No.	Grade	Down-town Area	Scores	Near Railway Station	Scores	Seas-hore	Scores
1.	Outstanding (5)	34	170	26	130	64	320
2.	Very good (4)	36	144	28	112	38	152
3.	Good (3)	42	126	58	174	42	126
4.	Average (2)	24	48	24	48	4	8
5.	Poor (1)	8	8	10	10	4	4
6.	No comment (0)	8	0	6	0	-	-
	Total	152	496	152	474	152	610

Source: Primary data.

Table 5.32 shows that the grading of the location of the hotels preferred by the foreign tourists reveals that 'Seashore' gets the first rank with 610 scores followed by 'Downtown area' with 496 scores and 'Near Railway station' with 474 scores respectively. It is clear from the table that the hotels are located as expected by most of the foreign tourists.

Domestic tourists' opinion about the area of hotels

To know about the opinion of domestic tourists regarding the area of the hotels, data have been gathered on six point scales. The aggregate points for each facility is computed and ranked in table 5.33.

It is observed from table 5.33 that in the case of domestic tourists, 'room area' gets the first position with 1142 scores followed by 'Restaurant' with 1072 scores, 'Parking Place' with 1042 scores, 'Seating capacity' with 1026 scores, 'Halls' with 906 scores, 'Health club' with 748 scores and 'Games court' with 526 scores. It is clear from the table that the facilities

'Health club' and 'Games court' have been very much relegated by domestic tourists.

Table 5.33: Domestic Tourists' opinion about the area of hotels

Sl.No.	Grade	Room Area	Score	Restau-rant	Score	Seating Capa-city	Score	Halls	Score	Park-ing Place	Score	Health club	Score	Games court	Score
1.	Appreciably adequate (5)	40	200	16	80	12	60	12	60	52	260	16	80	14	70
2.	More than adequate (4)	98	392	90	360	62	248	74	296	70	280	58	232	38	152
3.	Adequate (3)	168	504	182	546	198	594	118	354	132	396	70	210	42	126
4.	Less than adequate (2)	16	32	32	64	52	104	90	180	42	84	94	188	58	116
5.	Miserably adequate (1)	14	14	22	22	20	20	16	16	22	22	38	38	62	62
6.	No comment (0)	12	0	6	0	4	0	38	0	30	0	72	0	134	0
	Total	**348**	**1142**	**348**	**1072**	**348**	**1026**	**348**	**906**	**348**	**1042**	**348**	**748**	**348**	**526**

Source : Primary data.

Foreign tourists opinion about the area of hotels

In the opinion of foreign tourist, to know about the adequacy of the areas, data have been gathered on a six point scale. The aggregate points for each facility is computed and presented in table 5.34.

Table 5.34: Foreign Tourists' opinion about area of hotels

Sl.No.	Grade	Room Area	Score	Restau-rant	Score	Seating Capa-city	Score	Halls	Score	Park-ing Place	Score	Health club	Score	Games court	Score
1	2	3	4	5	6	7	8	9	10	11	12	13	14	15	16
1.	Appreciably adequate (5)	12	60	20	100	8	40	5	25	7	35	10	50	8	40
2.	More than adequate (4)	30	120	58	232	25	100	20	80	27	108	28	112	31	124

1	2	3	4	5	6	7	8	9	10	11	12	13	14	15	16
3.	Adequate (3)	55	165	35	105	50	150	30	90	45	135	56	168	50	150
4.	Less than adequate (2)	20	40	22	44	25	50	78	156	31	62	22	44	25	50
5.	Miserably adequate (1)	28	28	11	11	35	35	16	16	32	32	29	29	30	30
6.	No comment (0)	7	0	6	0	9	0	3	0	10	0	7	0	8	0
	Total	**152**	**413**	**152**	**492**	**152**	**375**	**152**	**367**	**152**	**372**	**152**	**403**	**152**	**394**

Source: Primary data.

It is observed from table 5.34 that in the case of foreign tourists, 'restaurant' gets the first position with 492 scores followed by 'room area' with 413 scores, 'health club' with 403 scores, 'games court' with 394 scores, 'seating capacity' with 375 scores, 'parking place' with 372 scores and 'halls' with 367 scores respectively.

Food habits

Food habits of the sample tourists are given in table 5.35.

Table 5.35: Food habits

Sl.No.	Veg./Non-Veg.	No. of Tourists	Percentage
1.	Vegetarian	100	20.00
2.	Non-Vegetarian	400	80.00
	Total	**500**	**100**

Source: Primary data.

The above table reveals that out of 500 tourists, 80 percent are non-vegetarians and the remaining 20 percent are vegetarians.

Domestic tourists' opinion about the prices charged

Table 5.36 shows the opinion of the domestic tourists about the prices charged by the hotels in Kanyakumari.

Table 5.36: Domestic tourists' opinion about the prices charged

Sl.No.	Grade	Room		Food		Beverage	
		No. of Tourists	Score	No. of Tourists	Score	No. of Tourists	Score
1.	Very high (5)	132	660	46	230	4	20
2.	High (4)	42	168	138	552	76	304
3.	Fair (3)	142	426	142	426	140	420
4.	Average (2)	22	44	10	20	100	200
5.	Low (1)	-	-	4	4	8	8
6.	No comment (0)	10	0	8	0	20	0
	Total	**348**	**1298**	**348**	**1232**	**348**	**925**

Source: Primary data.

Table 5.36 it is revealed that regarding the domestic tourists opinion about room tariff, majority 132 tourists consider that the room tariff is 'very high' with 660 scores followed by 'fair' with 426 scores, 'high' with 168 scores, 'average' with 44 scores. In the case of food tariffs, majority 138 domestic tourists consider food tariff to be 'high' with 552 scores followed by 'fair' with 426 scores, 'very high' with 230 scores, 'average' with 20 scores and 'low' with 4 scores. In the case of beverage tariff, majority 140 tourists consider beverage tariff was 'fair' with 420 scores followed by 'high' with 304 scores, 'average' with 200 scores and 'very high' with 20 scores. Overall, with 1,298 scores, room tariff is viewed to be too high followed by food tariff with 1,232 scores and Beverage tariff with 952 scores.

Foreign tourists' opinion about the prices charged

The opinions of the foreign tourists about the prices charged are given in the following table 5.37.

Table 5.37 reveals that majority 42 foreign tourists considered room tariff to be 'high' with 168 scores followed by 'very high' with 160 scores, 'fair' with 120 scores and 'average' with 56 scores. In the case of food, majority 42 foreign tourists considered food tariff to be 'high' with 120 scores followed by 'fair' with 114 scores, 'very high' with 100 score, and 'average' with 84 scores. In the case of 'beverage', majority 48 tourists considered beverage tariff to be 'fair' with 144 scores followed by 'high' with 120 scores, 'average' with 56 scores and 'very high' with 40 scores. The above table clearly reveals that on the whole the room tariff is viewed to be very high with 508 scores followed by food tariff with 434 scores and beverage tariff with 370 scores.

Table 5.37: Foreign tourists' opinion about the prices charged in Kanyakumari

Sl.No.	Grade	Room		Food		Beverage	
		No. of Tourists	Score	No. of Tourists	Score	No. of Tourists	Score
1.	Very high (5)	32	160	20	100	8	40
2.	High (4)	42	168	30	120	30	120
3.	Fair (3)	40	120	38	114	48	144
4.	Average (2)	28	56	42	84	28	56
5.	Low (1)	4	4	16	16	10	10
6.	No comment (0)	6	0	6	0	28	0
	Total	**152**	**508**	**152**	**434**	**152**	**370**

Source: Primary data.

Domestic tourists' opinions on the taste of food and beverage

The opinion of the domestic tourists about the taste of food and beverage is presented in table 5.38.

It is clearly seen from table 5.38 shows that domestic tourists are 'Indian food' is ranked first with 1182 scores followed by 'beverage' with 854 scores and 'continental food' with 842. In the case of 'Indian food' 'delicious' ranks first with 592 scores and 'Tasteless' ranks last with 28 scores. Regarding 'continental food' Tasty' ranks first with 396 scores and 'Tasteless' has the least scores of 92. In the case of 'beverages' 'Tasty' ranks first with 390 scores and 'Tasteless' ranks last with 38 scores.

Table 5.38: Domestic tourists' opinion about taste of food and beverage

Sl.No.	Grade	Indian Food		Continental Food		Beverage	
		No. of Tourists	Score	No. of Tourists	Score	No. of Tourists	Score
1.	More Delicious (5)	52	260	22	110	18	90
2.	Delicious (4)	148	592	28	112	48	192
3.	Tasty (3)	84	252	132	396	130	390
4.	Moderate(2)	22	44	66	132	72	144
5.	Tasteless (1)	28	28	92	92	38	38
6.	No comment (0)	14	0	8	0	42	0
	Total	**348**	**1,182**	**348**	**842**	**348**	**854**

Source: Primary data

Foreign tourists' opinion about the taste of food and beverage

Table 5.39 presents the opinion of the foreign tourists about food and beverage available in Kanyakumari hotels.

Table 5.39: Foreign tourists' opinion about the taste of food and beverage

Sl.No.	Grade	Indian Food		Continental Food		Beverage	
		No. of Tourists	Score	No. of Tourists	Score	No. of Tourists	Score
1.	Very Delicious (5)	22	110	20	100	14	70
2.	Delicious (4)	54	216	24	96	30	120
3.	Tasty (3)	28	84	50	150	58	174
4.	Moderate (2)	18	36	36	72	24	48
5.	Tasteless (1)	22	22	18	18	6	6
6.	No comment (0)	8	0	4	0	20	0
	Total	**152**	**468**	**152**	**436**	**152**	**418**

Source: Primary data.

It is clearly evident from the table 5.39 that foreign tourists are 'Indian food' is ranked first with 468 scores followed by continental food with 436 scores and 'beverage' with 418. In the case of 'Indian food' 'delicious' ranks first with 216 scores and 'Tasteless' ranks last with 22 scores. Regarding 'continental food' 'Tasty' ranks first with 150 scores and 'Tasteless' has the least scores of 18. In the case of 'beverages' 'Tasty' ranks first with 174 scores and 'Tasteless' ranks last with 6 scores.

Domestic tourists' opinion about décor, furnishing and furniture in hotels at Kanyakumari

Table 5.40 presents the domestic tourists' opinion about décor, furnishing and furniture in the hotels at Kanyakumari.

Table 5.40: Domestic tourists' opinion about décor, furnishing and furniture in the hotels

Sl. No.	Grade	No. of Tourists		All categories
		Star categories	Non-Star categories	
1.	Excellent	10 (7.04)	22 (10.68)	32 (9.20)
2.	Very good	22 (15.49)	36 (17.48)	58 (16.67)
3.	Good	32 (22.53)	66 (32.04)	98 (28.16)
4.	Average	42 (29.58)	48 (23.30)	90 (25.86)
5.	Poor	24 (16.90)	28 (13.59)	52 (14.94)
6.	No comment	12 (8.46)	6 (2.91)	18 (5.17)
	Total	**142 (100)**	**206 (100)**	**348 (100)**

Source: Primary data.

Note: Figures in brackets represent percentage to total.

From table 5.40 it is revealed that domestic tourists in the case of star category hotels 42 (29.58 percent) of the domestic tourists are of the opinion that the decor, furnishing and furniture are 'average' followed by 32 (22.53 percent) with the opinion 'good', 24 (16.90 percent) with the opinion 'poor'. In the case of non-star categories of hotels, majority of 66 (32.02 percent) of the domestic tourists opinion that the decor, furnishing and furniture are 'good' followed by 48 (23.30 percent) with the opinion 'average', 36 (17.48 percent) with the opinion 'very good' and 28 (13.59 percent) with the opinion 'poor'.

Foreign tourists' opinion about décor, furnishing and furniture in the hotels in Kanyakumari

The opinion of foreign tourists' about décor, furnishing and furniture in hotels in Kanyakumari are given in table 5.41.

Table 5.41: Foreign tourists' opinion about décor, furnishing and furniture in the hotels

Sl. No.	Grade	No. of Tourists		All categories
		Star categories	Non-Star categories	
1.	Excellent	4 (6.67)	8 (8.70)	12 (7.89)
2.	Very good	12 (20.00)	18 (19.57)	30 (19.74)
3.	Good	22 (36.67)	30 (32.04)	52 (34.21)
4.	Average	10 (16.67)	18 (19.57)	28 (18.42)
5.	Poor	4 (6.67)	6 (6.52)	10 (6.58)
6.	No comment	8 (13.32)	12 (13.03)	20 (13.16)
	Total	**60 (100)**	**92 (100)**	**152 (100)**

Source: Primary data.
Note: Figures in brackets represent percentage to total.

From table 5.41 it is observed that among the foreign tourists, in the case of star category hotels, majority of 22 (36.67 percent) are of the opinion that the decor, furnishing and furniture are 'good' followed by 12 (20.00 percent) with opinion 'very good'. 10 (16.67 percent) of the opinion 'average', 4 (6.67 percent) of the opinion 'excellent' and another 4 (6.67 percent) of the opinion are 'poor'. In the case of non-star category hotels, majority of 30 (32.04 percent) are the opinion that the décor, furnishing and furniture are 'good', followed by 18 (19.57 percent) with the opinion 'average' and another 18 (19.57 percent) are 'very good', 12 (13.03 percent) of had 'no comment' and 8 (8.70 percent) opined it to be 'excellent'.

Domestic tourists' opinion about the various services and facilities in star category hotels

Table 5.42 presents the opinion of domestic tourists about the various services and facilities in star category hotels.

Table 5.42: Domestic tourists' opinion about the various services and facilities in star category hotels

S. No.	Factors	Out standing (5)		Good (4)		Average (3)		Poor (2)		Very Poor (1)		Total Score	Weighted average score	Rank
		No. of Tourists		No. of Tourists		No. of Tourists		No. of Tourists		No. of Tourists				
1.	Rooms	88	440	138	552	98	294	22	44	2	2	1332	3.83	I
2.	Restaurant	42	210	102	408	170	510	33	66	1	1	1195	3.43	VIII
3.	Bar	62	310	128	512	150	450	8	16	-	-	1288	3.70	III
4.	Conference hall	52	260	142	568	138	414	14	28	2	2	1272	3.66	IV
5.	Shopping	48	240	138	552	146	438	13	26	3	3	1259	3.62	VI
6.	Staff	48	48	146	584	138	414	15	30	1	1	1269	3.64	V
7.	Laundry	58	290	138	552	90	270	60	120	2	2	1234	3.55	VII
8.	Telephone/ Telex	86	430	146	584	86	258	28	56	2	2	1330	3.82	II
9.	Others	48	240	90	360	174	522	34	68	2	2	1192	3.42	IX

Source: Primary data.
Note: Figures in brackets represent weightage.

It is inferred from table 5.42 that in the case of domestic tourists, among the various services and facilities in star category hotels, 'room' is ranked first with the highest weighted average score of 3.83, 'telephone/telex' is ranked second with the weighted average score of 3.82, 'bar' is ranked third with the weighted average score of 3.70, 'conference hall' is ranked fourth with the weighted average score of 3.66, 'staff' is ranked fifth with the weighted average score of 3.64, 'shopping' is ranked sixth with the weighted average score of 3.62, 'laundry' is ranked seventh with the weighted average score of 3.55, 'restaurant' is ranked eighth with the weighted average score of 3.43 and 'other facilities' is ranked last.

Foreign tourists' opinion about the various services and facilities in star category hotels

Table 5.43 reveals the foreign tourists' opinion about the various services and facilities in star category hotels.

Table 5.43: Foreign tourists' opinion about the various services and facilities in star category hotels

Sl. No.	Factors	Out standing (5)		Good (4)		Average (3)		Poor (2)		Very Poor (1)		Total Score	Weighted average score	Rank
		No. of Tourists		No. of Tourists		No. of Tourists		No. of Tourists		No. of Tourists				
1.	Rooms	22	110	62	248	48	144	18	36	2	2	540	3.55	VII
2.	Restaurant	32	160	78	312	32	96	9	18	1	1	587	3.86	III
3.	Bar	30	150	86	344	34	102	2	4	-	-	600	3.95	II
4.	Conference hall	38	190	80	320	30	90	2	4	2	2	606	3.99	I
5.	Shopping	34	170	74	296	28	84	15	30	1	1	581	3.82	IV
6.	Staff	22	110	56	224	38	114	33	66	3	3	517	3.40	IX
7.	Laundry	20	100	62	248	48	144	22	44	-	-	536	3.53	VIII
8.	Telephone/ Telex	28	140	70	280	38	114	15	30	1	1	565	3.72	V
9.	Others	30	150	58	232	50	150	12	24	2	2	558	3.67	VI

Source: Primary data.

Note: Figures in brackets represent weightage.

From table 5.43 it is inferred that in the case of foreign tourists, among the services and facilities in star category hotels, 'conference hall' is ranked first with the highest weighted average score of 3.99, 'bar' is ranked second with the weighted average score of 3.95, 'restaurant' is ranked third with the weighted average score of 3.86, 'shopping' is ranked fourth with the weighted average score of 3.82, 'telephone / telex' is ranked fifth with the weighted average score of 3.72, 'other facilities' are ranked sixth with the weighted average score of 3.67, 'rooms' is ranked seventh with the weighted average score of 3.56, 'laundry' is ranked eighth with the weighted average score of 3.53 and 'staff' is ranked last.

Average hotel expenses by the domestic and foreign tourists

The following table 5.44 shows the average hotel expenses by the domestic and foreign tourists.

Table 5.44: Average hotel expenses by the domestic and foreign tourists

Sl. No.	Amount in Rs.	Domestic Tourists	Percen-tage	Foreign Tourists	Percen-tage
1.	Below 1,000	165	47.41	6	3.95
2.	1,000-2,000	95	27.30	10	6.58
3.	2,000-3,000	20	5.75	18	11.84
4.	3,000 and above	68	19.54	118	77.63
	Total	**348**	**100**	**152**	**100**

Source: Primary data.

Table 5.44 shows the average hotel expenses of the domestic and foreign tourists. In the case of domestic tourists 165 (47.41 percent) tourists have spend below Rs.1,000, 95 (27.30 percent) tourists have spend Rs.1,000 to Rs.2,000, 20 (5.75 percent) have spend Rs.2,000 to Rs.3,000 and 68 (19.54 percent) tourists have spend above Rs.3,000 respectively. In the case of foreign tourists 6 (3.95 percent) have spent below Rs.1,000, 10 (6.58 percent) have spend Rs.1,000 to Rs.2,000, 18 (11.84 percent) have spend Rs.2,000 to Rs.3,000 and 118 (77.63 percent) tourists spent above Rs.3,000.

Opinion of the foreign tourists about actual expenditure

Opinion of the foreign tourists about the actual expenditure of foreign tourist is given in the following table 5.45.

The actual expenditure of most of the foreign tourists differs from their original plan of expenditure. The study reveals that 15.79 percent of the foreign tourists spend more than the amount budgeted for their visit, 64.47 percent of the tourists spend less than the amount budgeted and the remaining 19.74 of the foreign visitors spend exactly as planned by them.

Table 5.45: Opinion of the foreign tourists about actual expenditure

Sl.No.	Amount Spent	No. of Tourists	Percentage
1	More than planned	24	15.79
2	Less than planned	98	64.47
3	Exactly as planned	30	19.74
	Total	**152**	**100**

Source: Primary data.

Determinants of Expenditure of Tourists

This section is devoted to an identification of the factors which determine the expenditure of tourists with low income and high income on the one hand, and both the items taken together on the other. For this, the following multiple log-linear regression model was estimated separately for domestic and foreign tourists by the method of least squares.

$$\text{Log } Y = \beta_0 + \beta_1 \log X_1 + \beta_2 \log X_2 + \beta_3 \log X_3 + \beta_4 \log X_4 + u \qquad (5.1)$$

where,

Y = Total expenditure of tourists (in Rs.)

X_1 = Income of the tourists (in Rs.)

X_2 = Age (in years)

X_3 = Educational qualification

X_4 = Duration of stay (in numbers)

U = Disturbance term.

Estimated regression results of determinants of expenditure of tourists

The estimated results of the above model (5.1) are given in table 5.46 for domestic and foreign tourists.

Table 5.46: Estimated regression results of determinants of expenditure of tourists

Sl.No.	Variable	Parameters	Parameter Estimates	
			Domestic tourists	Foreign tourists
1.	Intercept	β_0	4.1172	3.7888
2.	Income	β_1	0.3042* (4.9651)	0.3242* (4.1121)
3.	Age	β_2	0.2536* (3.6737)	0.1942* (2.7814)
4.	Education	β_3	0.0243 (0.0472)	0.0341 (0.7148)
5.	Duration of Stay	β_4	0.2844* (3.4724)	0.2871* (3.1141)
6.	R2		0.6241	0.6147
7.	F-value		37.6412	39.4200
8.	No. of Observations		174	76

*Coefficients are statistically significant at 5 percent level.

Note: Figures in brackets represent t-value.

It is observed from table 5.46 that in the case of domestic tourists, the coefficient of multiple determination R^2 was 0.6241 indicating 62.41 percent variation in total expenditure with variables included in the regression model. The regression coefficient of variables namely, income, age and duration of stay were statistically significant at 5 percent level. It means that for one percent increase in these variables, the total expenditure could increase by 0.3042 percent, 0.2536 percent and 0.2844 percent respectively. Among the significant variables, income had a greater influence on the total expenditure. The F-value shows that the regression model fitted is statistically significant at one percent level.

In the case of foreign tourists, all the variables included in the model are jointly responsible for 61.47 percent variation in the total expenditure. The coefficient of income, age and duration of stay were found to be significant at 5 percent level and they were positively related to total expenditure. It indicates that one percent increase in these variables may lead to 0.3242 percent, 0.1942 percent and 0.2871 percent increase in the total expenditure respectively. It is revealed that the variable, income had a greater influence on the total expenditure of foreign tourists. As the F-value shows the regression model fitted is found to be significant at one percent level.

Summary

The findings of the analysis of the present chapter is summarised as follows:

Regarding the profile of the sample tourists, more than 68.39 percent of the domestic tourists belong to the age group of 25 to 40 years whereas in the case of foreign tourists this age group constituted more than 86.84 percent. Sex-wise classification indicates that the ratio of male and female was 70:30. The prominent mode of transport to Kanyakumari was government tourist vehicle. Most of the foreign tourists came to know about Kanyakumari from books on travel and tourism. Occupation-wise distribution showed that majority of the foreign tourists are professionals while in the case of domestic tourists, majority of them are business people. The purpose of both domestic and foreign tourists in coming over to Kanyakumari is for sightseeing and to fruitfully enjoy their leisure time.

Regarding hotel accommodation, domestic tourists prefer only economy type hotels while foreigners prefer deluxe room facilities. Majority of the foreign tourists and domestic tourists with high income prefer only Tamil Nadu hotels. The duration of stay was found high in the case of both domestic and foreign tourists.

The results of multiple log linear regression model showed that income, age and duration of stay have much influence on the expenditure of both domestic and foreign tourists.

CHAPTER

6

An Analysis Hotel Industry in the Study Area

Introduction

The core of hotel service lies in the full satisfaction of the tourists. Like any physical product, the services of star hotels are the offerings of the hoteliers as perceived by the tourists. Consumers perceive hotel service in terms of 'hotel image' and also in terms of the benefits and inconveniences that might result from its use.

Hotels play an important role in providing facilities for the transaction of business, meetings, conferences, recreation and entertainments. Locations, coupled with outstanding service, play a vital role in successfully pleasing the tourists.

Proximity to one's place of work cuts down on the business travellers' time, making all the difference, since tourists show concern about the status of the hotel room, tariff, etc., In most cases the important factors in room selection are the food quality and sufficiency in room service.

As the present study is related to star hotels and tourists, naturally, the tourists have a different perception about the services of star hotels as against the perception of tourists of non-star hotels.

Marketing both encompasses and addresses itself to the full range of human needs. As the human being ascends the ladder of needs, the input of marketing becomes more and more subtle, this is exactly applicable to the tourists preferring star hotels as they might have crossed all basic needs in the motivational ladder. The hoteliers have to find a strategies to satisfy esteem and self actualization needs of their tourists.[1]

It is obvious that a cup of coffee served in a star hotel, entails heavy cost, compared to the cost of one cup of coffee of similar quality offered in an ordinary hotel. Yet, a customer in a star hotel prefers to pay the high cost, provided he/she gets a bundle of satisfaction out of it. To generalize, a customer in a star hotel, who pays extraordinary costs for the products/ services would expect satisfaction of a unique nature.

A service is considered to be successful, only when it meets the unique satisfaction that the customer expects to derive from it. Unlike a person using a service facility in an ordinary hotel, a customer in a star hotel, gives much importance to 'Five Star Culture', 'Environment', 'Hospitality', 'Quality and taste' and 'Hygienic preparation' and so his/her unique satisfaction invariably hinges upon these factors.

In this chapter, an analysis is made on the various variables affecting the choice of hotels. Spotlights in this section include planned stay vs actual stay, preference of stay status, room types and plan types, ranking of hotel location and area, services of receptionist and boarding facilities. Further, marketing strategy for hotel services like product mix, product quality and promotional measures have also been discussed.

Marketing Strategy and Promotional Measures

In this section, the marketing functions such as selection of product mix determination of product quality and choosing promotional measures are discussed. The influence of seasons, the demand patterns, nature of target customers and method of booking rooms, average duration of stay of customers, the facilities available in star/non-star hotels and the various promotional measures undertaken by the hotels are presented. For the purpose of information to be gathered, 50 hotels were randomly selected.

Status of the hotels in Kanyakumari

Status of the hotels in Kanyakumari is given in the following table 6.1.

Table 6.1: Status of the hotel

Sl.No.	Status	No. of Hotels	Percentage
1.	Chain Hotel	14	28
2.	Affiliated Hotel	5	10
3.	Independent Hotel	31	62
	Total	**50**	**100**

Source: Primary data

Table 6.1 shows the status of the hotels in Kanyakumari. Out of 50 hotels, 14 (28 percent) hotels are chain hotels, 5 (10 percent) hotels are affiliated hotels and 31 (62 percent) are independent hotels.

Star category of hotels in Kanyakumari

Star category of the hotels in Kanyakumari is given in the following table 6.2.

Table 6.2: Star Category of Hotels

Sl. No.	Category of Hotels	No. of Hotels	Percentage
1.	1 Star Hotels	5	10
2.	2 Star Hotels	7	14
3.	3 Star Hotels	8	16
4.	Non-Star Hotels	30	60
	Total	**50**	**100**

Source: Primary data.

Table 6.2 shows the star category of the hotels in Kanyakumari. 5 (10 percent) hotels are one star hotels, 7 (14 percent) are two star hotels, 8 (16 percent) are three star hotels and 30 (60percent) are non-star hotels.

Total number of rooms in the hotels of Kanyakumari

The following table 6.3 shows the total number of rooms in all categories of hotels in Kanyakumari.

Table 6.3: Total number of rooms in the hotels of Kanyakumari

Sl.No.	Category of Hotels	No. of Hotels	Percentage
1	1 Star Hotels	129	6.68
2	2 Star Hotels	356	18.45
3	3 Star Hotels	586	30.36
4	Non-Star Hotels	859	44.51
	Total	**1930**	**100**

Source: Primary data.

The above table shows the total number of rooms in all categories of hotels in Kanyakumari. Out of 1930 rooms in all categories of hotels 129 (6.68 percent) rooms are in one star hotels, 356 (18.45 percent) are in two star hotels, 586 (30.36 percent) are in three star hotels and the remaining 859 (44.51 percent) rooms are in non-star category of hotels.

Category of rooms in the hotels of Kanyakumari

The following table 6.4 shows the total number of rooms in the categories of both star and non-star hotels.

Table 6.4: Category of rooms in the hotels of Kanyakumari

Sl.No.	Category of Hotels	No. of Hotels	Percentage
1.	Single bedded	35	1.81
2.	Double bedded	1344	69.64
3.	Three bedded	243	12.60
4.	Four bedded	196	10.15
5.	Five bedded	44	2.28
6.	Six bedded	58	3.00
7.	Eight bedded	6	0.31
8.	Twelve bedded	4	0.21
	Total	1930	100

Source: Primary data.

Table 6.4 shows the category of rooms in both star and non- star hotels in Kanyakumari 35 (1.81 percent) rooms are single bedded, 1344 (69.64 percent) rooms are double bedded, 243 (12.60 percent) rooms are three bedded, 196 (10.15 percent) rooms are four bedded, 44 (2.28 percent) rooms are five bedded, 58 (3 percent) rooms are six bedded, 6 (0.31 percent) and 4 (0.21 percent) rooms are eight and twelve bedded respectively.

Room pattern for Star Hotels

The room patterns for star hotels are of twenty two categories. They are single bedded deluxe A/C, and two bedded deluxe A/C to twelve bedded deluxe non A/C. The number of rooms, number of hotels and their mean value are given in the following table 6.5.

Table 6.5: Room pattern of star hotels

Sl.No.	Room types	No. of Rooms	No. of Hotels	Mean Average
1	2	3	4	5
1.	Single bedded deluxe A/c	20	3	6.67
2.	2 bedded deluxe A/c	124	9	13.78
3.	2 bedded executive suite A/c	14	5	2.80
4.	2 bedded standard A/c	118	6	19.67
5.	2 bedded standard Non A/c	103	10	10.30
6.	2 bedded deluxe Non A/c	143	10	14.30
7.	2 bedded semi deluxe Non A/c	29	2	14.50
8.	2 bedded sea-facing A/c	135	7	19.29
9.	2 bedded sea-facing Non A/c	70	5	14.00
10.	2 bedded luxury A/c	18	3	6.00
11.	3 bedded deluxe A/c	55	11	5.00
12.	3 bedded deluxe Non A/c	75	14	5.36
13.	3 bedded standard Non A/c	32	8	4.00
14.	3 bedded deluxe sea-facing A/c	14	6	2.33
15.	3 bedded deluxe sea-facing Non A/c	28	5	5.60

1	2	3	4	5
16.	4 bedded deluxe A/c	26	12	2.16
17.	4 bedded deluxe sea-facing Non A/c	32	13	2.46
18.	5 bedded deluxe A/c	7	4	1.75
19.	5 bedded deluxe sea-facing Non A/c	9	6	1.5
20.	6 bedded standard Non A/c	10	4	2.5
21.	8 bedded standard Non A/c	6	2	3.00
22.	12 bedded deluxe Non A/c	4	2	2.00
	Total	**1071**		

Source: Primary data.

Table 6.5 it is observed that the highest mean of 19.67 is seen for two bedded standard A/C rooms followed by 19.29 mean average for two bedded sea-facing A/C rooms, 14.50 mean average for two bedded semi deluxe Non A/C room, mean average of 14.30 for two bedded deluxe non A/C rooms, 14 mean average for two bedded sea-facing non A/C rooms, 13.78 mean average for two bedded deluxe A/C rooms, 10.30 mean average for two bedded standard non A/C rooms and 6.67 mean average for single bedded deluxe A/C room. The lowest mean average of 1.5 is for five bedded deluxe sea-facing room A/C. Majority of the star hotels have the room types of two bedded A/C and non A/C rooms.

Room pattern for non-star hotels in Kanyakumari

The following table 6.6 shows the room patterns in non-star hotels. There are twenty categories of rooms available in the non-star hotels of Kanyakumari. These are single bedded ordinary A/C, two bedded deluxe A/C, two bedded deluxe non A/C, two bedded standard non A/C, two bedded standard A/C to six bedded ordinary non A/C.

Table 6.6 reveals the room pattern of non-star hotels in Kanyakumari. The highest mean average of 5.42 is found for two bedded ordinary non A/C followed by the mean average of 4.86 for two bedded deluxe suite non A/C, mean average

Table 6.6: Room pattern for non-star hotels

Sl. No.	Room types	No. of Rooms	No. of Hotels	Mean Average
1.	Single bedded ordinary A/c	15	4	3.75
2.	2 bedded deluxe A/c	35	18	1.94
3.	2 bedded deluxe Non A/c	48	22	2.18
4.	2 bedded standard A/c	54	24	2.25
5.	2 bedded standard Non A/c	65	21	3.09
6.	2 bedded semi deluxe Non A/c	22	8	2.75
7.	2 bedded deluxe suite Non A/c	34	7	4.86
8.	2 bedded suite A/c	15	8	1.87
9.	2 bedded ordinary A/c	115	28	4.11
10.	2 bedded ordinary Non A/c	141	26	5.42
11.	2 bedded deluxe sea-facing A/c	28	8	3.5
12.	2 bedded deluxe sea-facing Non A/c	34	10	3.4
13.	3 bedded ordinary A/c	15	11	1.36
14.	3 bedded ordinary Non A/c	24	14	1.71
15.	4 bedded deluxe A/c	30	10	3.00
16.	4 bedded deluxe Non A/c	38	12	3.16
17.	4 bedded ordinary A/c	22	18	1.22
18.	4 bedded ordinary Non A/c	48	22	2.10
19.	5 bedded ordinary Non A/c	28	12	2.33
20.	6 bedded ordinary Non A/c	48	14	3.42
	Total Rooms	**859**		

Source: Primary data.

of 4.11 for two bedded ordinary A/C, 3.75 mean average for single bedded ordinary A/C, mean average of 3.50 for two bedded deluxe sea-facing A/C, mean average of 3.42 for six bedded ordinary non A/C and mean average of 3.40 for two bedded deluxe sea-facing non A/C rooms. The lowest mean average is 1.22 for four bedded ordinary non A/C rooms. Majority for the non-star hotels have the room types of two bedded A/C and non A/C rooms.

Tariff for star hotels during peak and off seasons

The tariff for star hotels is divided into two categories. One during peak or full season and other during off seasons. The mean average of peak and off season tariffs for twenty star hotels in Kanyakumari is given in the table 6.7.

Table 6.7: Tariff for star hotels during peak and off seasons

Sl. No.	Room types	Mean Average (Peak Seasons) (in Rs.)	Mean Average (Off Seasons) (in Rs.)
1.	Single bedded deluxe A/c	2500	2037.50
2.	2 bedded deluxe A/c	2258.60	1818.30
3.	2 bedded executive suite A/c	4182	3210
4.	2 bedded standard A/c	2060	1645
5.	2 bedded standard Non A/c	1151.70	793.10
6.	2 bedded deluxe Non A/c	1531.80	763.60
7.	2 bedded semi deluxe Non A/c	1261.30	1900
8.	2 bedded deluxe sea-facing A/c	2687.50	1856.30
9.	2 bedded sea-facing Non A/c	1662.50	1400
10.	2 bedded luxury A/c	4900	3650
11.	3 bedded deluxe A/c	2464	1225
12.	3 bedded standard Non A/c	900	550
13.	3 bedded standard Non A/c	1396.70	833
14.	3 bedded deluxe sea-facing A/c	3900	1900
15.	3 bedded deluxe A/c	1500	1300
16.	4 bedded deluxe A/c	3162.50	2262.50
17.	4 bedded deluxe A/c	1852.70	1475
18.	4 bedded deluxe Non A/c	1607.50	1366.60
19.	4 bedded semi deluxe Non A/c	3250	1450
20.	4 bedded deluxe A/c	2020	1675
21.	5 bedded deluxe A/c	2500	1780
22.	5 bedded deluxe sea-facing Non A/c	3000	2250
23.	6 bedded standard Non A/c	3750	1265
24.	8 bedded standard Non A/c	2950	2070
25.	12 bedded deluxe Non A/c	3325	2875

Source: Primary data.

Table 6.7 it is observed that during peak seasons the highest tariff mean average is Rs.4,900 for two bedded luxury A/C room followed by the mean average of Rs.4,182 for two bedded executive suite A/C, the mean average of Rs.3,900 for three bedded deluxe sea-facing A/C rooms, the mean average Rs.3,750 for six bedded standard non A/C, the mean average Rs.3,325 for twelve bedded deluxe non A/C, mean average of Rs.3,250 for four bedded semi deluxe non A/C and mean average of Rs.3,162.50 for four bedded deluxe A/C rooms. The lowest tariff mean average of Rs.900 is found for three bedded deluxe non A/C rooms.

Regarding the tariff for star hotels during off seasons, the highest tariff mean average of Rs.3,650 is found for two bedded luxury A/C rooms followed by the mean average of Rs.3,210 for two bedded executive suite A/C rooms, mean average of Rs.2,875 for twelve bedded deluxe non A/C, mean average of Rs.2,262.5 for four bedded deluxe A/C, mean average of Rs.2,250 for five bedded deluxe sea-facing non A/C, mean average of Rs.2,070 for eight bedded standard non A/C and mean average of Rs.2,037.50 for single bedded deluxe A/C rooms. The lowest tariff mean average of Rs.550 is found for three bedded deluxe non A/C rooms.

Tariff for non-star hotels during peak and off seasons in Kanyakumari

The following table 6.8 shows the mean average of tariff for non-star hotels during peak and off seasons in Kanyakumari.

It is seen from the table 6.8 that regarding the tariff for non-star hotels during peak seasons, the highest mean average of Rs.2,600 is found for four bedded deluxe A/C rooms, followed by the mean average of Rs.1,933.30 for two bedded standard A/C, mean average of Rs.1,718.80 for two bedded deluxe A/C and mean average of Rs.1,662.50 for single bedded ordinary A/C rooms. The lowest mean average tariff of Rs.452.90 is found for two bedded ordinary non A/C rooms.

Regarding the of tariff for non-star hotels during off seasons, the highest mean average of Rs.1, 712.50 is found for four bedded deluxe A/C rooms followed by a mean average of Rs.1, 650 for two bedded standard A/C rooms, mean average of Rs.1, 250 for two bedded deluxe sea-facing A/C rooms, mean average of Rs.1, 225 for single bedded ordinary A/C rooms and mean average of Rs.1, 212.50 for two bedded deluxe A/C rooms. The lowest mean average tariff of Rs.261.80 is found for two bedded ordinary non A/C rooms.

Table 6.8: Tariff for non-star hotels during peak and off seasons in Kanyakumari

Sl. No.	Room types	Mean Average (Peak Seasons) (in Rs.)	Mean Average (Off Seasons) (in Rs.)
1.	Single bedded ordinary A/c	1662.50	1225
2.	2 bedded deluxe A/c	1718.80	1212.50
3.	2 bedded deluxe Non A/c	631.70	391.70
4.	2 bedded standard A/c	1933.30	1650
5.	2 bedded standard Non A/c	1062.50	737.50
6.	2 bedded deluxe semi Non A/c	1150	750
7.	2 bedded deluxe suite Non A/c	1275	912.50
8.	2 bedded deluxe suite A/c	1487.50	1187.50
9.	2 bedded ordinary A/c	816.70	566.70
10.	2 bedded ordinary Non A/c	452.90	261.80
11.	2 bedded deluxe sea-facing A/c	1525	1250
12.	2 bedded deluxe sea-facing Non A/c	816.60	500
13.	3 bedded ordinary A/c	1450	1125
14.	3 bedded ordinary Non A/c	827.10	462.50
15.	4 bedded deluxe A/c	2600	1712.50
16.	4 bedded deluxe Non A/c	766.70	516.70
17.	4 bedded ordinary A/c	1500	1100
18.	4 bedded ordinary Non A/c	808.80	500
19.	5 bedded ordinary Non A/c	850	525
20.	6 bedded ordinary Non A/c	1235.70	857.10

Source: Primary data.

Total number of beds in the hotels of Kanyakumari

The total number of beds in both star and non-star hotels in Kanyakumari is given in the table 6.9.

Table 6.9: Total number of beds in the hotels of Kanyakumari

Sl.No.	Category of Hotels	No. of Beds	Percentage
1.	1 Star	708	13.94
2.	2 Star	828	16.31
3.	3 Star	1321	26.02
4.	Non-star	2220	43.73
	Total	**5077**	**100**

Source: Primary data.

It is seen from the above table, that there are 708 (13.94 percent) beds in one star hotels. 828 (16.31 percent) beds in two star hotels, 1321 (26.02 percent) beds in three star hotels and 2220 (43.73 percent) beds in non-star hotels in Kanyakumari.

Seasonality

The room occupancy in hotels mostly depends on 'seasons'. The season may be lean, normal and peak. During peak season, the inflow of tourists is high because of the favourable weather conditions to the foreign tourists. Usually, peak season is in the months of October, November, December and January.

Nature of season for star and non-star hotels

The nature of tourist seasons for star and non-star categories of hotels is given in the following table 6.10.

Table 6.10: Nature of season for star and non-star hotels in Kanyakumari

Sl.No.	Nature of Season	No. of Hotels	Percentage
1.	Normal throughout the year	15	30
2.	Peak throughout the year	4	8
3.	Combination of peak and normal	31	62
	Total	**50**	**100**

Source: Primary data.

The above table shows the nature of season for the star hotels and non-star in Kanyakumari. The majority of 31 (62 percent) hotels enjoy the combination season of peak and normal, 15 (30 percent) enjoy normal season throughout the year and 4 (8 percent) hotels have peak season throughout the year.

Lean season for star category hotels

The following table 6.11 shows the lean season for star categories of hotels.

Table 6.11: Lean season for star category hotels

Sl.No.	Lean Season	No. of Months	No. of Hotels	Percentage
1.	February - April	3	5	25
2.	May - July	3	11	55
3.	August - September	2	3	15
4.	No Lean Season	-	1	5
	Total		**20**	**100**

Source: Primary data.

Table 6.11 reveals that among star hotels. 5 (25 percent) hotels have the lean season from February to April, 11 (55 percent) hotels from May to July, 3 (15 percent) have the lean season from August to September and 1 (5 percent) hotel has no lean season at all.

Lean season for Non-star Categories of Hotels

The lean season for non-star categories of hotels, in Kanyakumari is classified in to four categories namely February to April, May to July, August to September and no lean season as given in the following table 6.12.

Table 6.12 reveals that 10 (33.33 percent) non-star hotels have the lean season from February to April, 15 (50 percent) hotels have the lean season from May to July, 2 (6.67 percent) have the lean season from August to September and the remaining 3 (10 percent) hotels have no lean season at all.

Table 6.12: Lean season for non-star categories of hotels in Kanyakumari

Sl.No.	Lean Season	No. of Months	No. of Hotels	Percentage
1.	February - April	3	10	33.33
2.	May - July	3	15	50.00
3.	August - September	2	2	6.67
4.	No Lean Season	—	3	10.00
	Total		**30**	**100**

Source: Primary data.

Average Room Occupancy during lean Season in Star Categories of hotels in Kanyakumari

The following table 6.13 shows the average room occupancy of star hotels during lean season in Kanyakumari.

Table 6.13: Average room occupancy during lean season in star category hotels in Kanyakumari

Sl.No.	Room Occupancy (%)	No. of Hotels	Percentage
1.	51-52	2	10
2.	53-54	1	5
3.	55-56	2	10
4.	57-58	4	20
5.	59-60	11	55
	Total	**20**	**100**

Source: Primary data.

It is clearly understood from the above table that out of 20 star hotels, 2 (10 percent) hotels show 51-52 percent room occupancy, 1 (5 percent) hotel 53-54 percent, 2 (10 percent) hotels 55-56 percent, 4 (20 percent) hotels 57-58 percent and 11 (55 percent) hotels, show 59-60 percent room occupancy.

Average room occupancy during lean season for non-star categories of hotels in Kanyakumari

The average room occupancy during lean season for non-star categories of hotels is given in the following table.

Table 6.14: Average room occupancy during lean season for non-star categories of hotels in Kanyakumari

Sl.No.	Room Occupancy (%)	No. of Hotels	Percentage
1.	61 – 62	2	6.67
2.	63 – 64	6	20.00
3.	65 – 66	7	23.33
4.	67 – 68	4	13.33
5.	69 – 70	11	36.67
	Total	**30**	**100**

Source: Primary data.

The above table shows the average room occupancy during lean season for non-star hotels. Out of 30 hotels, 2 (6.67 percent) hotels show 61-62 percent of room occupancy, 6 (20 percent) hotels have 63-64 percent, 7 (23.33 percent) hotels have 65-66 percent, 4 (13.33 percent) hotels have 67-68 percent and the remain 11 (36.67 percent) hotels have 69-70 percent room occupancy.

Normal season for star categories of hotels in Kanyakumari

The following table 6.15 shows the normal seasons for star categories of hotels in Kanyakumari. The normal seasons are divided into five categories namely December to March, January to March, February to April, April to August and no normal season at all.

Table 6.15: Normal season for star categories of hotels in Kanyakumari

Sl.No.	Normal Season	No. of Months	No. of Hotels	Percentage
1.	December – March	4	11	55
2.	January – March	3	3	15
3.	February – April	3	2	10
4.	April – August	5	3	15
5.	No normal season	-	1	5
	Total	**-**	**20**	**100**

Source: Primary data.

It is inferred from table 6.15 that 11 (55 percent) star hotels have the normal demand during December to March, 3 (15 percent) hotels during January to March, 2 (10 percent) hotels have normal demand during February to April, 3 (15 percent) hotels during April to August and the remaining 1 (5 percent) hotel has no normal season in a year.

Normal season for non-star categories of hotels in Kanyakumari

Normal season for non-star categories of hotels is given in the following table 6.16.

Table 6.16: Normal season for non-star categories of hotels in Kanyakumari

Sl.No.	Normal Season	No. of Months	No. of Hotels	Percentage
1.	January – March	3	13	43.33
2.	December – March	4	6	20.00
3.	March – August	6	4	13.33
4.	March – July	5	5	16.67
5.	No normal period	—	2	6.67
	Total		**30**	**100**

Source: Primary data.

The above table shows the normal season for non-star categories of hotels in Kanyakumari.13 (43.33 percent) non-star hotels have the normal demand during January – March, 6 (20 percent) during December to March, 4 (13.33 percent) during March – August, 5 (16.67 percent) during March-July and 2 (6.67 percent) hotels have no normal season in a year.

Average room occupancy of star categories of hotels during normal season

The following table 6.17 shows the average room occupancy of star categories of hotels in Kanyakumari during normal season.

Table 6.17 clearly exhibits the average room occupancy during normal season in star categories of hotels in

Kanyakumari. 2 (10 percent) star hotels have the room occupancy of 71-72 percent, 4 (20 percent) hotels 73-74 percent, 1 (5 percent) hotel 75-76 percent, 3 (15 percent) hotels 77-78 percent and 10 (50 percent) hotels have room occupancy of 79-80 percent.

Table 6.17: Average room occupancy of star categories of hotels during normal season

Sl.No.	Room Occupancy (%)	No. of Hotels	Percentage
1.	71-72	2	10
2.	73-74	4	20
3.	75-76	1	5
4.	77-78	3	15
5.	79-80	10	50
	Total	**20**	**100**

Source: Primary data.

Average room occupancy during normal season of non-star categories of hotels in Kanyakumari

The following table 6.18 shows the average room occupancy of non-star hotel categories during normal season in Kanyakumari.

Table 6.18: Average room occupancy during normal season for non-star categories of hotels in Kanyakumari

Sl.No.	Room Occupancy (%)	No. of Hotels	Percentage
1.	76-77	9	30.00
2.	78-79	7	23.33
3.	80-81	5	16.67
4.	82-83	6	20.00
5.	84-85	3	10.00
	Total	**30**	**100**

Source: Primary data.

It is evident from the above table that out of 30 non-star hotels, 9 (30 percent) hotels have the room occupancy of 76-77 percent, 7 (23.33 percent) hotels have the room occupancy of 78-79 percent, 5 (16.67 percent) hotels have the room occupancy of 80-81 percent, 6 (20 percent) hotels have the room occupancy of 82-83 percent and the remaining 3 (10 percent) hotels have the room occupancy of 84-85 percent.

Peak season for star category of hotels in Kanyakumari

The following table 6.19 shows the peak season for star category of hotels in Kanyakumari. The peak season is classified into five categories namely season throughout year, October – December, November to January, December to March and March to May.

Table 6.19: Peak season for star category of hotels in Kanyakumari

Sl. No.	Peak Season	No. of Months	No. of Hotels	Percentage
1.	Throughout the year	12	3	15
2.	October – December	3	7	35
3.	November – January	3	6	30
4.	December – March	4	2	10
5.	March – May	3	2	10
	Total		**20**	**100**

Source: Primary data.

Table 6.19 it is observed that out of 20 star categories of hotels 3 (15 percent) have peak season throughout the year, 7 (35 percent) hotels have peak season for 3 months in a year i.e., from October to December, 6 (30 percent) hotels have peak season for 3 months in a year i.e., from November to January 2 (10 percent) hotels have 4 months from December to March and 2 (10 percent) hotels have 3 months of peak season from March to May.

Peak season for non-star Categories of Hotels

Peak season for non-star categories of hotels is given in the following table 6.20.

Table 6.20: Peak season for non-star categories of hotels in Kanyakumari

Sl.No.	Peak Season	No. of Months	No. of Hotels	Percentage
1.	Throughout the year	12	3	10.00
2.	October – December	3	8	26.67
3.	November – January	3	10	33.33
4.	December – April	5	7	23.33
5.	March - May	3	2	6.67
	Total	-	**30**	**100**

Source: Primary data.

It is seen from the above table that 3 (10 percent) non-star hotels have peak season throughout the year, 8 (26.67 percent) have peak season for 3 months in a year i.e., October to December, 10 (33.33 percent) hotels have peak season for 3 months in a year from November to January, 7 (23.33 percent) hotels have peak season for 5 months in a year from December – April and 2 (6.67 percent) hotels have peak season for 3 months i.e., from March - May.

Average room occupancy of star categories of hotels during peak season

The following table 6.21 shows the average room occupancy of star categories of hotels in Kanyakumari during peak season.

Table 6.21: Average room occupancy during peak season for star categories of hotels in Kanyakumari

Sl.No.	Room Occupancy (%)	No. of Hotels	Percentage
1.	91 – 92	2	10
2.	93 – 94	3	15
3.	95 – 96	3	15
4.	97 – 98	4	20
5.	99 – 100	8	40
	Total	**20**	**100**

Source: Primary data.

Table 6.21 reveals that all 20 star categories of hotels in Kanyakumari, to achieve more than 90 percent occupancy during peak season. In fact 15 out of 20 star hotels are able to attain occupancy ranging between 95-100 percent.

Average room occupancy of non-star categories of hotels in Kanyakumari during peak season

Average room occupancy during peak season for non-star categories of hotels is given in the following table 6.22.

Table 6.22: Average room occupancy of non-star categories of hotels in Kanyakumari during peak season

Sl.No.	Room Occupancy (%)	No. of Hotels	Percentage
1.	91 – 92	2	6.67
2.	93 – 94	3	10.00
3.	95 – 96	7	23.33
4.	97 – 98	8	26.67
5.	99 – 100	10	33.33
	Total	**30**	**100.00**

Source: Primary data.

From table 6.22 it is inferred that the average room occupancy of non-star categories of hotels, during peak season is more than 90 percent. In fact, 25 out of 30 such hotels are able to attain average room occupancy ranging between 95-100 percent.

Annual Average Room Occupancy

The annual room occupancy is classified into two categories, namely, annual average room occupancy in the year 2008 -09 and percentage of annual room occupancy in the year 2008-2009.

Annual average occupancy of rooms during 2008-09

The following table 6.23 shows the annual average occupancy of rooms in kanyakumari during 2008-09.

An analysis of the annual average occupancy of hotel rooms indicates that the number of room occupied is below

10,000 per annum in the case of 26 percent of the hotels. It ranges between 10,000 – 20,000 rooms per annum in the case of 6 percent of the hotels, 20,000-30,000 rooms in the case of 22 percent of the hotels, 30,000-40,000 rooms in the case of 14 percent of the hotels, 40,000-50,000 rooms in the case of 18 percent of the hotels and 50,000-60,000 in the case of 8 percent of the hotels. The room occupancy of 2 percent of the hotels is between 70,000 – 80,000 rooms and that of 4 percent of hotels ranges between 80,000 – 90,000 rooms per annum.

Table 6.23: Annual average occupancy of rooms in Kanyakumari hotels during 2008-09

Sl.No.	No. of Rooms Occupied per annum	No. of Hotels	Percentage
1.	Below 10,000	13	26
2.	10,000 – 20,000	3	6
3.	20,000 – 30,000	11	22
4.	30,000 – 40,000	7	14
5.	40,000 – 50,000	9	18
6.	50,000 – 60,000	4	8
7.	70,000 – 80,000	1	2
8.	80,000 – 90,000	2	4
	Total	**50**	**100**

Source: Primary data.

Percentage of annual room occupancy in the hotels of Kanyakumari during 2008-09

The percentage of annual room occupancy during 2008-09 is given in table 6.24.

The annual average room occupancy ratio of the 50 hotels surveyed, shows that the room occupancy of 2 hotels is between 76-80 percent, that of 13 hotels is between 81-85 percent, that of 9 hotels is between 86-90 percent, that of another 7 hotels is between 91-95 percent and that of the remaining 19 hotels ranges between 96-100 percent.

Table 6.24: Percentage of annual room occupancy during 2008-09

Sl.No.	No. of Rooms Occupied per annum	No. of Hotels	Percentage
1.	76 – 80	2	4
2.	81 – 85	13	26
3.	86 – 90	9	18
4.	91 – 95	7	14
5.	96 – 100	19	38
	Total	**50**	**100**

Source: Primary data.

Annual room occupancy

The following table shows the annual room occupancy for period of six years from 2003-04 to 2008-09.

Table 6.25: Annual room occupancy in the hotels of Kanyakumari

Sl.No.	Occupancy (in %)	Year					
		2003-04	2004-05	2005-06	2006-07	2007-08	2008-09
		Number of Hotels in percentage					
1.	66 – 70	12	8	4	2	—	—
2.	71 – 75	14	12	6	4	2	—
3.	76 – 80	16	14	12	10	8	2
4.	81 – 85	24	18	24	22	22	26
5.	86 – 90	22	20	14	16	14	16
6.	91 – 95	12	24	20	18	14	18
7.	96 – 100	—	4	20	28	40	38
	Total	**100**	**100**	**100**	**100**	**100**	**100**

Source: Primary data.

Nearly half-a-decade ago, the star hotels with less than 75 percent occupancy ratio accounted for 26 percent. However, the ever increasing demand for hotel rooms has caused these hotels to improve their occupancy ratio with the result of which only 2 percent of the hotels had the occupancy ratio of less than 75 percent during 2008-09. It is to be stressed that not even a single hotel at present is short of 75 percent occupancy ratio.

The steady increase in the number of hotels achieving more than 90 percent occupancy ratio in the last 6 years is a pointer, exposing the effect of internal growth of tourism coupled with the over-whelming need for hotels by the foreign tourists in India. In the year 2003-04, only 12 percent of the star hotels enjoyed an occupancy ratio of 91-95 percent and in 2008-09, 18 percent of star hotels were able to achieve an occupancy ratio of 91-95 percent. In addition, to this, 38 percent of hotels achieved an occupancy ratio of 96-100 percent.

As already pointed out, at the end of 2009, the total number of rooms available in star hotels in India was be 39,287 (including hotels awaiting classification) as against an estimated room requirements of 59,000. This phenomenon is more pronounced in the case of star hotels in South India. The actual number of rooms in star hotels in South India is far less than the estimated room requirement of hotels. According to the President of South Indian Hoteliers Association, the estimated shortage of rooms in South Indian Star hotels would be nearly 6,000.

It is very clear that the demand for rooms outnumbers the supply of rooms. In other words, the hotel industry enjoys sellers' market where shortage of rooms makes them dominate the market.

Annual average bed Occupancy

The annual average bed occupancy ratio of the 50 hotels surveyed, shows that the percentage of bed occupancy of most of the hotels ranges between 51-55to76-80 percent as given in the table 6.26.

Table 6.26 shows that the annual average bed occupancy of both star and non-star categories of hotels in Kanyakumari. In the case of star hotels majority 9 hotels have a bed occupancy of 56-60 percent, 4 hotels with 66-70 percent, 3 hotels with 61-65 percent, 2 hotels with 71-75 percent and the bed occupancy of one hotel is 51-55 percent and another one is 76-80 percent.

Table 6.26: Percentage of annual average bed occupancy in the hotels of Kanyakumari

Sl.No.	Bed Occupancy (%)	No. of star hotels	No. of non-star hotels	Total	Percentage
1.	51 – 55	1	2	3	6
2.	56 – 60	9	5	14	28
3.	61 – 65	3	8	11	22
4.	66 – 70	4	8	12	24
5.	71 – 75	2	5	7	14
6.	76 – 80	1	2	3	6
	Total	**20**	**30**	**50**	**100**

Source: Primary data.

In the case of non-star hotels majority 8 hotels have the bed occupancy of 61-65 percent, another 8 hotels have 66-70 percent, 5 hotels have 56-60 and another 5 hotels 71-75 percent, 2 hotels have bed occupancy of 51-55 and another two 76-80 percent.

Modes of Booking Rooms in Star and Non-star Hotels

Regarding the modes of booking rooms in both star and non-star hotels, generally, five methods such as spot booking, advance booking by the tourists, booking through travel agents, booking through e-mail and booking through friends/ relatives are followed.

Modes of booking rooms in star and non-star hotels in Kanyakumari

Modes of booking rooms in star and non-star hotels are given in the below table.

The above table shows that the modes of booking rooms differ among star categories. As far as One to three star hotels are concerned, 64 percent of tourists book on the spot, for 12 percent booking is done in advance booking by the tourists themsevels, 10 percent through agents, 6 percent through e-mail and the remaining 8 percent through friends/relatives.

Table 6.27: Modes of booking rooms in star and non-star hotels

Sl.No.	Source of Booking	Star Categories (in Percent)	Non-Star Categories (in Percent)
1.	Spot Booking	64	72
2.	Advance booking by the tourists	12	7
3.	Booking through agents	10	5
4.	Booking through e-mail	6	3
5.	Booking through friends / Relatives	8	13
	Total	**100**	**100**

Source: Primary data.

In the case of non-star hotels 72 percent of tourists book rooms on the spot, 7 percent in advance by the tourists themselves, 5 percent through agents, 3 percent through e-mail and the remaining 13 percent booking rooms is through friends/relatives.

Modes of booking rooms for domestic and foreign tourists

The following table 6.28 shows the modes of booking rooms in star and non-star hotels adopted by both domestic and foreign tourists Garrett ranking technique has been adopted and the results are show in the following table.

Table 6.28: Modes of booking rooms for domestic and foreign tourists

Sl. No.	Mode of Booking	Domestic tourists		Foreign tourists	
		Mean Score	Rank	Means Score	Rank
1.	Spot Booking	54.66	1	55.43	1
2.	Advance booking by the tourists themselves	50.22	2	53.45	2
3.	Through Agent	47.93	4	47.17	4
4.	Through e-mail	47.89	5	47.96	3
5.	Through Friends/ Relatives	49.31	3	45.99	5

Source: Primary data.

Table 6.28 clearly exhibits the modes of booking rooms in star and non-star hotels by domestic and foreign tourists. In case of domestic tourists, among all the modes of booking rooms 'spot booking' is ranked first with the highest mean score of 54.66, 'advance booking by customers' is ranked second with the mean score of 50.22, 'booking through friends/relatives' is ranked third with the mean score of 49.31, 'booking through agent' is ranked fourth with the mean score of 47.93 and 'booking through e-mail' is ranked last with the mean score of 47.89.

In the case of foreign tourists 'spot booking' ranks first with the mean score of 55.43, 'advance booking by the tourists' ranks second with the mean score of 53.45, 'booking through mail' ranks third with the mean score of 47.96, 'booking through agent' ranks fourth with the mean score of 47.17 and 'booking through friends/relatives' ranks last with the mean score of 45.99.

Type of Occupants

The occupants of a hotel may be domestic tourists or foreign tourists. The foreign occupants are classified into foreign tourist occupants in star hotels and foreign tourist occupants in non-star hotels.

Foreign tourists occupants in star hotels

The following table 6.29 shows the number of foreign tourist occupants in star hotels.

Table 6.29: Foreign tourist occupants in star hotels

Sl.No.	Occupants (%)	No. of Hotels	Percentage
1.	30-35	4	20
2.	35-40	2	10
3.	40-45	6	30
4.	45-50	8	40
	Total	**20**	**100**

Source: Primary data.

It is seen from the above table that in the case of star categories of hotels, the percentage of foreign tourist occupants in 4 out of 20 hotels, is 30-35 percent, 35-40 percent in 2 hotels, 40-45 percent in 6 hotels and 45-50 percent in the remaining 8 hotels.

Foreign tourist occupants in non-star hotels

The following table 6.30 shows the number of foreign tourist occupants in non-star hotels.

Table 6.30: Foreign tourist occupants in non-star hotels

Sl.No.	Occupants (%)	No. of Hotels	Percentage
1.	1-10	11	36.67
2.	10-20	8	26.67
3.	20-30	5	16.66
4.	30-40	6	20.00
	Total	**30**	**100**

Source: Primary data.

Table 6.30 shows the number of foreign tourist occupants in non-star hotels. In non-star categories of hotels, the percentage of foreign tourist occupants in 11 out of 30 hotels is less than 10 percent, in 8 hotels it is 10-20 percent, in 5 hotels it is 20-30 percent and in the remaining 6 hotels it is 30-40 percent.

The point to be noted here is that in all the non-star hotels, 1-40 percent of their occupants are foreign tourists, whereas, in most of the non-star hotels (80 percent) foreign tourists constitute less than 30 percent only.

Cuisine Offered in the Star Hotels

The star hotels in India have to be very responsive in offering the food items that would be relished by people from different states and countries. The cuisine offered by the star hotels like Indian food, Continental food, Chinese food, Vegetarian and French, Italian, Thai, Mughal Tandori, etc., are given in table 6.31.

Table 6.31: Cuisine offered by Star Hotels

Sl.No.	Cuisine	National Level*			Hotels Surveyed		
		Total No. of Hotels	Total No. of Hotels Offering Cuisine	Percentage	Total No. of Hotels	Total No. of Hotels Offering Cuisine	Percentage
1.	Indian	413	376	89	50	41	82
2.	Continental	413	361	87	50	36	72
3.	Chinese	413	191	70	50	32	64
4.	Vegetarian	413	61	14	50	9	18
5.	Others	413	122	30	50	5	10

***Source:** Data compiled from the book entitled "Hotels and Restaurant Guide India 2009", Published by Federation of Hotel and Restaurant, Associations of India.

It is found from table 6.31 that at the national level, Indian cuisine offered by 89 percent of the star hotels, continental food by 87 percent hotels, Chinese by 70 percent hotels, vegetarian food by 14 percent hotels and other food items such as French, Italian, Thai, Mughal Tandori, etc., are offered by 30 percent of the hotels.

The present study also reveals a more or less same pattern as regards the cuisine offered in the star hotels of Kanyakumari. The variety of food available in the star hotels surveyed include Indian food in 82 percent hotels, continental in 72 percent hotels, Chinese in 64 percent hotels, vegetarian in 18 percent and other food items in 10 percent of the hotels surveyed for this study.

Promotional Methods Adopted

"Promotion is persuasive in that it attempts to move . people from a stage of unawareness to one of awareness, from liking to preference, or from conviction to purchase".[2] It includes both direct and indirect communication and encompasses personal selling, advertising, publicity and public relation, and sales promotion.

Promotional methods adopted by star hotels in Kanyakumari

The promotional methods adopted by star hotels are press advertisement, sign boards, Posters, Instant reservation facilities, sales calls, network facilities, sales conferences and public relations. The following table shows the promotional methods of star hotels.

Table 6.32: Promotional methods adopted by star hotels in Kanyakumari

Sl.No.	Methods	No. of Hotels	Percentage
1.	Press Advertisement, Sign Boards, Posters and Instant reservation facilities	3	15
2.	Press Advertisement, Sign Boards, Posters, Instant reservation, Network and Sales Calls	5	25
3.	Press Advertisement, Sign Boards, Posters, Instant reservation, Network, Sales Calls and Sales Conferences	8	40
4.	Press Advertisement, Network, Sales Calls Sales Conferences and public relation	4	20
	Total	**20**	**100**

Source: Primary data.

The study makes an analysis of the different promotional methods followed by the hotels. 15 percent of the 20 star hotels use press advertisements, sign boards, poster and instant reservation. 25 percent use press advertisements, sign boards, posters, instant reservation, network and sales calls. 40 percent of the hotels have different promotional methods such as press advertisement, sign boards, posters, instant reservation, network, sales calls and sales conferences and the remaining 20 percent use press advertisement, network, sales calls, sales conferences and public relation as promotional methods.

It is to be noted that not even a single star hotel has been taking efforts to improve public relations.

A pleasant and confident smile and smart appearance do a tremendous amount of public relations for a hotel and it is this first pleasant sight that sets the mood of the customer. Politeness is an integral part of hotel service and undivided attention its concomitant. Courtesy at the counter is judged by attentiveness, interest, tone of voice and appearance and behaviour.

Promotional methods of non-star hotels

The following table 6.33 shows the promotional methods adopted by non-star hotels.

Table 6.33: Promotional methods adopted by non-star hotels

Sl.No.	Methods	No. of Hotels	Percentage
1.	Press Advertisement, Sign Boards, Posters and Instant reservation facilities	9	30
2.	Press Advertisement, Sign Boards, Posters, Instant reservation, Network and Sales Calls	13	43.33
3.	Press Advertisement, Sign Boards, Posters, Instant reservation, Network, Sales Calls and Sales Conferences	6	20
4.	Press Advertisement, Network, Sales Calls and Sales Conferences and public relation	2	6.67
	Total	**30**	**100**

Source: Primary data.

It is seen from table 6.33 that in the case of non-star hotels, 30 percent use presses advertisements, sign boards, posters and instant reservation as sales promotional methods. 43.33 percent of the hotels use press advertisement, sign boards, posters, instant reservation, sales calls and network, 20 percent adopt sales conference along with the measures as stated above and the remaining 6.67 percent adopt public relation along with other measures like press advertisement, network, and sales conference.

Credit Cards

Credit card plays a vital role in this dynamic world. It is safe, convenient and easy to effect payment up to Rs.20,000 by means of credit card. The card takes care of a customer's travel and stay, entertainment and shopping needs. A large number of prestigious establishments such as hotels, airlines, railways, shops, restaurants, stores, hospitals across the country are now accepting credit cards.

Recognizing the indispensable benefits arising out of credit cards, large hotel-chains offer their own credit cards. The credit cards accepted by star hotels are shown.

Table 6.34: Credit Cards Accepted by Star Hotels

Sl.No.	Credit Card	National Level*			Hotels Surveyed		
		Total No. of Hotels	No. of Hotels accep-ting	Percen-tage	Total No. of Hotels	No. of Hotels accep-ting	Percen-tage
1.	Dinner's Club	413	260	62.95	50	26	50.83
2.	Visa Card	413	205	49.63	50	20	39.16
3.	American Express Card	413	196	47.45	50	15	30.00
4.	Central Card	413	183	44.30	50	19	38.33
5.	Master Card	413	163	39.46	50	16	32.50
6.	Bob Card	413	155	37.53	50	13	25.00
7.	Andhra Bank Card	413	120	29.05	50	18	35.00
8.	Can Card	413	155	37.53	50	21	40.83
9.	Mercard	413	83	20.09	50	11	21.66

Source: Data compiled from the book entitled "Hotels and Restaurant Guide India 2009", Published by Federation FHRA of India.

Table 6.34 shows that 85 percent of the 413 approved star hotels are accepting credit cards. In practice, large hotels accept different varieties of credit cards. An analysis is made as to the type of credit cards accepted by all star hotels in India. It reveals that nearly nine types of cards are mostly accepted (in addition to other cards) by the hotels.

At the national level, 63 percent of the 413 star hotels accepts Diner's Club Card, 50 percent accept Visa Card, 44 percent Central Credit Cards, 47 percent American Express Cards, 39 percent Master Card, 38 percent each Bob Card and Can Card, 29 percent Andhra Bank Card and 20 percent of the hotels accept Mercard.

The survey also shows more or less the same pattern as regards the credit cards accepted by users in Kanyakumari star and non-star hotels. 80 percent of the 50 hotels accept credit cards. The variety of cards accepted by star and non-star hotels includes Diner's Club (51 percent), Cancard (41 percent), Visa (39 percent), Central Card (38 percent), Andhra Bank (35 percent), American Express (30 percent), Master Card (33 percent), Bobcard (25 percent) and Mercard (22 percent).

Facilities Available in Star Hotels

The following facilities are generally available the star hotels in Northern and Western regions:

Convention Halls, Banquet Halls, Meeting Halls, Conference Rooms, Committee Rooms, Party Rooms, Executive Club Rooms, Business Centres, Threatre, Secretarial Service, Simultaneous translation in different languages, Exhibition Area, Discotheque, Restaurants, Outside catering, Bar, Coffee Shop, Room Service, Tax Free Shop, Pantry Shop, Tea Lounge, India & Indian Airlines Sales & Reservation Office, Airline Counter and Office, International Travel and Tour Counters, Travel Agents and Tour Operators, Courtesy Transport from Domestic & International Airports to the hotels, Car Rental, Library, News Service, International Newspapers & Periodicals, Bank, Post and Telegraph Office, Safe Deposit Lockers, Credit Cards, Money Changing facilities, Courier Service, Teleprinter, Telex-24 Hours, Running Hot & Cold water, Laundry & Dry cleaning, Valet, Barber shop, Steam Bath, Bathroom Telephone, Doctor on call, Wheel chair, Games Court, Health Club, Swimming Pool etc.

However, it is observed that the hotels in South India have been providing nearly 70 percent of these facilities.

REFERENCES

1. Maurice I. Mandell and Larry J. Rosenberg, Mrketing, Prentice Hall of India Pvt. Ltd., New Delhi, 1983, Second edition, p. 186.
2. Rom J. Markin, *Marketing*, John Wiley & Sons, New Work, 1999, p. 445.

CHAPTER 7

Summary of Findings, Suggestions and Conclusion

Introduction

The hotel industry constitutes one of the vital and essential components of tourist industry. The tourist industry, in other words, is also termed as leisure industry, while hotel industry is termed as hospitality industry. It goes without saying that this hospitality industry provides services such as accommodation, food and beverages, not only to those travelling for pleasure, but also to the business travellers. By doing so, the hotel industry, as a whole, benefits from increased travel. It has, therefore, been aptly said "No Hotels, No Tourism".

Findings of The Study

In keeping with the first objective, an elaborate study was undertaken in Chapter III about the major tourist centres in Kanyakumari district. No pain was spared in giving a vivid portrayal of the environmental significance of tourist attractions such as forests, waterfalls, landscapes, monuments of ancient civilization like Kumari Amman Temple, Bhagavathi Amman Temple, Vivekananda Memorial, Gandhi Memorial, Suchindram Temple, Udayagiri Fort, Padmanabhapuram Palace, Mathoor Thotti Palam, and the like in Chapter III. This chapter shows how the natural, cultural and social environments of regions are a major lure for both national and international tourists.

The second objective was examined in Chapter IV. A steady increase was observed in the arrivals of domestic as well as foreign tourists in Tamil Nadu and Kanyakumari during the period of study.

The tourist arrival in Tamil Nadu from the year 1999-2000 to 2008-2009 was examined and it was found that majority i.e., 20.50 percent of the tourists arrived during the year 2008-09 and 4.83 percent of tourists arrived during 2006-07. This reveals a steady increase in the tourist arrival. In India, Tamil Nadu state ranks first in domestic and foreign tourist arrival. Among domestic and foreign tourists in Kanyakumari, majority i.e., 13.76 percent have arrived during the year 2008-09. The lowest percent of 5.94 tourist have arrived during the year 2004-05. The tourist arrival in Kanyakumari shows a relatively stable trend of growth during the period of study.

The average tourist arrival during the period from 1999-2000 to 2008-2009 was found to be 39274230 in Tamil Nadu and 1688363 in Kanyakumari. The co-efficient of variation of foreign tourists in Kanyakumari was found to be higher. The fluctuations in domestic and total tourist arrivals in Tamil Nadu were found to be high compared to Kanyakumari.

It could be seen that the highest percent of 13.80 domestic and foreign tourists arrived in Kanyakumari in the month of January and 12.15 percent tourists in the month of May. The lowest 4.82 percent of tourists arrived in the month of July.

In the present study, seasonal variations in the tourist arrival for 10 years have been found applying the moving average method. For domestic tourists the highest percent of 166.16 is found during the month of January and the lowest percent of 57.60 during the month of July. Regarding foreign tourists, the highest percent of 132.50 is found during the month of January and the lowest percent of 75.15 during the month of July.

Regarding the irregular indices of tourist arrival in Kanyakumari from 2000 to 2009, for domestic tourists the highest percent of 113.31 was found for the month of May, followed by 112.32 percent for the month of December and the lowest percent of 95.14 for the month of March. Regarding foreign tourists, the highest percent of 113.26 was seen during the month of December followed by 112.24 percent for the month of April and the lowest percent of 98.61 for the month of February.

It could be seen that the trend co-efficient of domestic and foreign tourist arrival is positive and statistically significant at 5 percent level. It indicates that the arrival of domestic and foreign tourists have gone up at the rate 2.3679 percent and 2.0016 percent per annum. The growth rates for domestic and foreign tourist arrival are 4.091 percent and 6.07 percent respectively.

Regarding the third objective, namely demand and supply of hotel accommodation, the analysis revealed that there are three different classifications namely first class, second class, third class and low class of rooms based on the tariff charged by hotels.

The trend in the growth of different types of hotels in the study area was analysed and it was found that the value of trend co-efficient is higher for first class hotels (0.08), second (0.09), third (0.03) and low class (0.04) hotels. Regarding the growth rate of boarding and lodging units in Kanyakumari during the period from 2003 to 2009, the growth rate is higher among the second class hotels, followed by first class, low class and third class hotels.

Regarding the total bed capacity available per day in all the four classes of hotels, out of 1870 rooms, the highest number of 1344 rooms are (71.87 percent) double bedded and the remaining 526 (28.13 percent) rooms are three, four and five bedded.

It is inferred that the highest bed capacity of 4812 beds was found in the year 2009. 4605 beds in the year 2008 and the lowest bed capacity of 3393 beds was found in the year

2003. The beds available in Kanyakumari are found to have been steadily increasing year by year.

While studying the demand and supply of beds for both domestic and foreign tourists, it was found that the demand for beds is less than the supply of beds during the period of study in Kanyakumari. It indicates that there the demand for beds is more than of the supply and the excess demand varies from 679 in 2003 to 1203 in 2009.

It could be understood that the trend co-efficient of demand and supply of beds is statistically significant at 5 percent level and are positive. It indicates that the demand and supply of beds has steadily increased at the rate of 0.114 percent and 0.118 percent respectively per annum. The growth rates of demand and supply of beds are 12.09 percent and 12.63 percent respectively.

The fourth objective of the study was to bring out in detail the expenditure portfolio and its basic determinants with respect to the sample tourists in Kanyakumari.

Out of 500 tourists, 348 (69.60 percent) are Indians and 152 (30.40 percent) are foreign tourists. Among the foreign tourists, tourists from Sri Lanka and Malaysia stayed for an average duration of 12 and 11 days respectively and tourists from France stayed for the least average duration of 4 days.

The age group of 25-35 years composed nearly 50 percent of the total tourists and those above 40 years composed nearly 8 percent of the total tourists in Kanyakumari. Sex-wise classification showed that male tourists constituted 70 to 73 percent, while female tourists only 27 to 30 percent. Majority of the domestic tourists are married constituting 75.29 percent and 24.71 percent tourists are unmarried. Among foreign tourists 64.47 percent are married and 35.53 percent are unmarried.

Among domestic tourists 193 (55.46 percent) are graduates and 75 (21.55 percent) are post graduates. The lowest number of 20 (5.74 percent) have completed only school level. In the case of foreign 68 (44.74 percent) tourists are post graduates, 52 (34.20 percent) are professional degree holders and only 2

(1.32 percent) belong to the category of school level. It may be inferred that domestic as well as foreign tourists are well educated.

Among the domestic tourists, 92 (26.44 percent) have private employment followed by 82 (23.56 percent) who are business men and 24 (6.90 percent) who are agriculturalists. In the case of foreign tourists, 58 (38.15 percent) have private employment, 45 (29.61 percent) tourists are professionals and the least number of 10 (6.58 percent) tourists are students. Out of 348 domestic tourists, 166 (47.70 percent) tourists earn Rs.10,000 to Rs.25,000 and 95 (27.30 percent) tourists earn Rs.25,000 to Rs.50,000 and the lowest number of 42 (12.07 percent) tourists are earn below Rs.10,000. Among foreign tourists, 75 (49.34 percent) tourists earn Rs.75, 000 to Rs.1, 00,000. 33 (21.71 percent) tourists earn above Rs.1, 00,000 and the lowest number of tourists 16 (10.53 percent) earn below Rs.50, 000.

While analysing the factors that influence the domestic tourists to visit Kanyakumari, it was found that 112 domestic tourists are influenced by relatives and 22 tourists are influenced by tour guide books. In the case of foreign tourists, 68 tourists are influenced by tour guide books, 30 tourists by non-Indian tour operators and the least number of 6 tourists are influenced by Indian tour operators.

While studying the position of Kanyakumari in the travel itinerary, it was found that among domestic tourists for 280 (80.46 percent) tourists it is their first destination and only 68 (19.54 percent) it is an extension tour from other parts of India. In the case of foreign tourists, for 120 (78.96 percent) tourists it is an extension tour from other parts of India and for 16 (10.52 percent) tourists it is their first destination.

Out of 348 domestic tourists, 268 (77.01 percent) tourists are using their own car / tourist car. Among the foreign tourists 80 (52.63 percent) tourists are using government tourist vehicles. Regarding the opinion of domestic and foreign tourists about the mode of transport availed, 'flight' ranked first with the weighted average score of 4.33 and rated to be highly expensive, 'ship' ranked second with the weighted average score of 2.76 and rated to be expensive. Bus is ranked last with the weighted average score of 1.25 and rated to be cheap.

The most delightful tourism activity in Kanyakumari for domestic tourists is visiting the 'religious places' and is ranked first with the, highest mean score of 56.47 and 'traditional and cultural values' ranked last with the mean score of 44.29. In the case of foreign tourists the most delightful activity is 'boating' and is ranked first with the highest mean score of 57.47 and 'religious places' ranked last with the mean score of 46.95.

It is inferred from the analysis, that 161 respondents (46.26 percent) arrange the tour themselves and only 22 (6.32 percent) tourists arrange the tour through travel agents. In the case of foreign tourists, majority of 90 (59.21 percent) tourists arrange the tour by travel agents and the lowest number of 4 (2.63 percent) tourists through friends/relatives.

Among the total respondents, for 254 (72.99 percent) domestic tourists and 130 (85.53 percent) foreign tourists annual programmes of leisure (sight seeing) is the major purpose for the tours. The lowest numbers of 4 (1.15 percent) domestic tourists and 4 (2.63 percent) foreign tourists have visited Kanyakumari for health purpose.

It is inferred from the analysis that out of 500 tourists, majority i.e., 210 (42 percent) tourists have their source of information about hotels of stay from travel agents and the least number of 40 (8 percent) tourists from tourist guides.

An analysis of the modes of transport used by the tourists to reach the hotels of their stay revealed that 186 (37.20 percent) tourists use car and the least number of 30 (6 percent) tourists use company coaches.

Regarding the average number of days of stay of foreign tourists in India, it was found that out of the 152 foreign tourists, the highest number of 59 (38.82 percent) tourists stayed for 20-30 days and the lowest 14 (9.21 percent) tourists stayed in India for 1-10 days and 40-50 days. As for the actual stay as against the original plan of foreign tourists, 86 (56.58 percent) have stayed in India less than the proposed number of days and the least number of 22 (14.47 percent) foreign tourists have stayed in India for more than the proposed number of days.

Regarding the domestic tourists' preference to the category of hotels, 174 (50 percent) tourists preferred non-star hotels and the lowest number of 26 (7.47 percent) tourists' preferred three star hotels. In the case of foreign tourists, majority, i.e., 82 (53.95 percent) tourists' preferred three star hotels and the lowest number of 10 (6.58 percent) tourists preferred non-star hotels.

While analysing the reasons for selection of one to three star hotels by foreign tourists, it was found that 82 (57.75 percent) tourists feel that the cost is not commensurating with the benefit and the least number of 8 (5.63 percent) tourists gave the reason of facing difficulties in advance booking. As for the tourists' preference to the plan types, out of 500 tourists 340 tourists prefer European plan and only 34 tourists prefer other plans like package plan and off seasonal concession plan.

The fifth objective of the study was to examine the tourists' evaluation of hotel facilities and services in Kanyakumari.

In selection of rooms, quality of food, hotel image, hospitality of workers, room service quality and room tariff are the most important factors whereas health club, swimming pool facilities, etc., are the least significant factors.

Regarding the tourists preference to the types of rooms major number of 258 (51.60 percent) tourists preferred to stay in single bedded room and the least number of 40 (8 percent) tourists preferred suites.

Among the factors influencing hotel choice among domestic tourists 'hotel image' is ranked first with the highest weighted average score of 4.09. 'Workers hospitality' is ranked second with the weighted average score of 4.02. 'Games court' is ranked the last with the weighted average of 1.91. Among foreign tourists, the factors, 'hotel image' is ranked first with the highest weighted average score of 4.01, 'food quality' is ranked second with the weighted average score of 3.95 and 'games court' is ranked last with the weighted average score of 1.99.

It is observed that out of 500 tourists, 264 (52.80 percent) tourists are booking rooms through direct sport booking and 60 (12 percent) tourists through company, travel departments, travel club, friend, etc.

Regarding the location of hotels, among the domestic tourists, 'down town area' gets the first rank with 1202 scores and 'located near railway station' gets the last rank with 1162 scores. Among the foreign tourists 'near seashore' gets the first rank with 610 scores and 'near railway station' gets the last rank with 474 scores.

Regarding the opinion about the area of hotels in the case of domestic tourists, 'room area' gets the first position with 1142 scores and 'games court' gets the last position with 526 scores. In the case of foreign tourists, 'restaurant' gets the first position with 492 scores and 'halls' gets the last position with 367 scores.

Majority of the respondents, i.e., 400 (80 percent) are non-vegetarians and 100 (20 percent) are vegetarians. The opinion of the domestic tourists about the prices charged is that the overall room tariff is high which has 1298 scores, followed by food tariff with 1232 scores and beverage tariff with 952 scores.

Among the foreign tourists the factor room rent is high ranks first, with 508 scores followed by food tariff with 434 scores and beverage tariff with 370 scores.

It could be observed from the analysis that Indian food is ranked first, by the domestic tourists, with 1182 scores and continental food is ranked last with 842 scores. Indian food is ranked first, by the foreign tourists with 468 scores and beverage is ranked last with 418 scores.

Regarding the opinion about decor, furnishing and furniture in star category hotels 42 domestic tourists (29.58 percent) felt it was 'average' followed by the least number of

10 (7.04) of tourists whose opinion was 'excellent'. In the non-star category hotels 66 (32.04 percent) of the tourists opinion was 'good' and the least number of 6 (2.91 percent) of the tourists' opinion was 'no comment'.

It could be seen that the highest 36.67 percent of the foreign tourists' opinion about décor, furnishing and furniture in star category was 'good' and that the lowest 6.67 percent was 'excellent' and another 6.67 percent was 'poor'. Regarding the furnishing in the non-star category hotels the highest 32.04 percent of tourists had the opinion 'good' and the lowest 6.52 percent tourists had the opinion 'poor'.

It is evident from the study that in the case of domestic tourists regarding the various services and facilities in star category hotels, 'room' is ranked first with the highest weighted average score of 3.83, 'telephone/telex' is ranked second with the weighted average score of 3.82 and 'other facilities' is ranked last with the weighted average score of 3.42. Among foreign tourists, 'conference hall' is ranked first with the highest weighted average score of 3.99 and 'staff' is ranked last with the weighted average score of 3.40.

Regarding the average amount spent per day by the domestic tourists, it was found that 90 (26.86 percent) tourists spend between Rs.1,000 to Rs.1,250 and the least number of 20 (5.75 percent) tourists spend between Rs.1,500 to Rs.2,000. The average hotel expenses of 165 (47.41 percent) domestic tourists is below Rs.1,000, that of 95 (27.30 percent) tourists is Rs.1,000 to Rs.2,000 and of 20 (5.75 percent) tourists between Rs.2,000 to Rs.3,000. In the case of foreign tourists, 118 (77.63 percent) tourists spend Rs.3,000 and above and 6 (3.95 percent) tourists spend below Rs.1,000.

The results of multiple log linear regression model showed that income, age and duration of stay have much influence on the expenditure of both domestic and foreign tourists.

Out of 50 hotels, 31 (62 percent) hotels are independent hotels, 14 (28 percent) hotels are chain hotels and 5 (10 percent) hotels are affiliated hotels.

Out of the hotels in Kanyakumari, majority i.e., 30 (60 percent) are non-star hotels, 8 (16 percent) are three star hotels, 7 (14 percent) are two star hotels and only 5 (100 percent) hotels are one star hotels respectively.

The total number of rooms in all categories of hotels in Kanyakumari is 1930 in all categories of hotels. Out of this 859 (44.5 percent) rooms are in non-star hotels, 586 (30.36 percent) are in three star hotels and the least number of 129 (6.68 percent) rooms are in one star hotels.

It was found that among the different categories of rooms in both star and non-star hotels in Kanyakumari, 1344 (69.64 percent) rooms are double bedded and only 4 (0.21 percent) rooms are twelve bedded.

Regarding room pattern for star hotels the highest mean of 19.67 is seen for two bedded standard A/C rooms and the lowest mean average of 1.5 is for five bedded deluxe sea-facing non A/C rooms. It is revealed in the room pattern of non-star hotels in Kanyakumari, the highest mean average of 5.42 is found for two bedded ordinary non A/C followed by the mean average of 4.86 for two bedded deluxe suite A/C and the lowest mean average of 1.22 for four bedded ordinary non A/C rooms. Regarding the tariff for star hotels during peak seasons, the highest tariff mean average of Rs.4,900 for two bedded luxury A/C rooms followed by the mean average of Rs.4,182 for two bedded executive suite A/C. The lowest tariff mean average of Rs.900 is found for three bedded deluxe non A/C rooms. Regarding the tariff for star hotels during off seasons, the highest tariff mean average of Rs.3,650 is found for two bedded luxury A/C rooms. The lowest tariff mean average of Rs.550 is found for three bedded deluxe non A/C rooms.

It could be observed from the analysis of the tariff for non-star hotels during peak seasons, the highest mean average of Rs.2, 600 is found for four bedded deluxe A/C rooms. The lowest mean average tariff of Rs.452.90 is found for two bedded ordinary non A/C rooms. Regarding the tariff for non-star hotels during off seasons, the highest mean average of Rs.1, 712.50 is found for four bedded deluxe A/C rooms. The lowest mean average tariff of Rs.261.80 is found for two bedded ordinary non A/C rooms.

As for the total number of beds in the hotels of Kanyakumari, more number i.e., 2,220 (43.73 percent) beds are in non-star hotels and only 708 (13.94 percent) beds are in one star hotels.

Regarding the analysis of the nature of season for the star and non-star hotels in Kanyakumari, the majority of 31 (62 percent) hotels enjoy the combination season of peak and normal, 15 (30 percent) enjoy normal season throughout the year and only 4 (8 percent) hotels have peak season throughout the year.

It is inferred from the analysis on the lean season for star category hotels, that 11 (55 percent) hotels have the lean season from May to July and only 1 (5 percent) hotel has no lean season at all. As for the lean season for non-star category of hotels 15 (50 percent) hotels have the lean season from May to July and only 2 (6.67 percent) have the lean season from August to September.

It is observed from the analysis on the average room occupancy during lean season in star category hotels in Kanyakumari, that out of 20 star hotels 11 (55 percent) hotels show 59-60 percent room occupancy and only one (5 percent) hotel shows 53-54 percent room occupancy. In the case of non-star categories of hotels, out of 30 hotels, the highest number of 11 (36.67 percent) hotels have 69-70 percent room occupancy and the least number of 2 (6.67 percent) hotels have 61-62 percent of room occupancy.

It was found from the analysis on the normal season for star categories of hotels in Kanyakumari, that majority of 11 (55 percent) star hotels have the normal demand during December to March and only one (5 percent) hotel has no normal season in a year. In non-star categories of hotels in Kanyakumari, majority of 13 (43.33 percent) non-star hotels have the normal demand during January to March and only 2 (6.67 percent) hotels have no normal season in a year.

It is evident from the analysis on the average room occupancy of star categories of hotels during normal season that 10 (50 percent) hotels have 79-80 percent room occupancy and only one (5 percent) hotel has 75-76 percent room occupancy. Among non-star hotels, 9 (30 percent) hotels have the room occupancy of 76-77 percent and only 3 (10 percent) hotels have the room occupancy of 84-85 percent.

It is observed from the analysis on the peak season for star category of hotels in Kanyakumari, that out of 20 star categories of hotels, 7 (35 percent) hotels have peak season for 3 months in year i.e., from October to December, 2 (10 percent) hotels have 4 months from December to March and another 2 (10 percent) hotels for 3 months of peak season from March to May. Among the non-star hotels, 10 (33.33 percent) hotels have peak season for 3 months in a year, from November to January and only 2 (6.67 percent) hotels have peak season for 3 months i.e., from March to May.

The analysis on the average room occupancy during peak season for star categories of hotels in Kanyakumari reveals that all 20 star categories of hotels have achieved more than 90 percent occupancy during peak season. 15 out of 20 star hotels are able to attain occupancy ranging between 95-100 percent. The average room occupancy of non-star categories of hotels, during, peak season is more than 90 percent. 25 out of 30 such hotels are able to attain average room occupancy ranging between 95-100 percent.

Regarding the annual average occupancy of hotel rooms in Kanyakumari during 2008-09, it is seen that in 13 (26 percent) hotels the number of rooms occupied is below 10,000 rooms per annum followed by 11 (22 percent) hotels, where the number of rooms occupied was between 20,000 to 30,000 rooms per annum and only one (2 percent) hotel had the number of rooms occupied, between 70,000 to 80,000.

It was found from the analysis on the annual room occupancy during the period from 2003 - 04 to 2008-09, that the star hotels with less than 75 percent occupancy ratio, accounted for 26 percent. Only 2 percent of the hotels had the occupancy ratio of less than 75 percent during 2008-09.

Regarding the modes of booking rooms in star hotels. 64 percent of the tourists book on the spot, 12 percent booking is done in advance by the tourist themselves and only 6 percent book through e-mail. In the case of non-star hotels, 72 percent of the tourists book rooms on the spot and only 3 percent book through e-mail.

It is evident from the study that among the modes of booking rooms in star and non-star hotels by domestic tourists, 'spot booking' is ranked first with the highest mean score of 54.66, 'advance booking by the tourist themselves is ranked second with the mean score of 50.22 and 'booking through e-mail' is ranked last with the mean score of 47.89. In the case of foreign tourists 'spot booking' ranks first with the mean score of 55.43, 'advance booking by the tourist themselves' ranks second with the mean score of 53.45 and 'booking through friends/relatives' ranks last with the mean score of 45.99.

It is inferred that among the foreign tourist occupants in star categories of hotels, majority i.e., 8 (40 percent) hotels have occupancy of 45-50 percent and that least number of 2 (10 percent) hotels the occupancy is 35-40 percent. Regarding the non-star categories of hotels, majority i.e., 11 (36.67 percent) hotels have occupancy is 1-10 percent, and the least number of 5 (16.66 percent) hotels the occupancy is 20-30 percent.

The analysis for the cuisine offered by star hotels at the national level, revealed that Indian cuisine was offered by 89 percent of the star hotels, continental food by 87 percent, Chinese by 70 percent and vegetarian food by the least 14 percent hotels. In the star hotels of Kanyakumari, Indian food is offered in 82 percent hotels, continental food in 72 percent hotels, Chinese food in 64 percent hotels and the other food items in the least 10 percent hotels.

The study reveals the promotional methods adopted by star hotels. Out of 20 star hotels 8 (40 percent) hotels use press advertisements, sign boards, posters, instant reservation facilities, network, sales calls and sales conferences and only

3 (15 percent) hotels use press advertisements, sign boards, posters and instant reservation facilities. Out of the 30 non-star hotels, 13 (43.33 percent) use press advertisements, sign boards, posters, instant reservation, network and sales calls and only 2 (6.67 percent) hotels adopt public relation along with other measures like press advertisements, network and sales conferences.

It is inferred from the analysis on the credit cards accepted by star hotels at the national level, that 63 percent of the 413 star hotels accept Diner's Club card, 50 percent accept Visa Card, 44 percent Central Credit Card and that least 20 percent of the hotels accept Mercard. In Kanyakumari among both star and non-star hotels 80 percent of the 50 hotels accept credit cards. Majority i.e., 51 percent hotels accept Diner's club Card, 41 percent accept Visa Card and the least 22 percent hotels accept Mercard.

Suggestions and Policy Recommendations

It is quite heartening to know that hotel industry has recently been recognized by the government as one of the major industries. The hotel industry has yet to be treated as an industry, in the right sense of the term. To put it more bluntly, hotel business (industry) is not considered as an industry fully and fairly in India whenever concessions and incentives are provided to various other industries. However, it is quite disheartening to note that hotel business is very much treated as 'industry' for the purpose of levying taxes.

Keeping all the problems connected with hotel and tourism industries in the country, in general and in Kanyakumari, in particular the researcher has made the following suggestions and recommendations applicable both at the national and micro-levels. The first few recommendations are meant for the country as a whole and the rest are to be adopted to the hotel and tourism industries in Kanyakumari.

1. Hotel and tourism industries should, first of all, be treated as infant industries and provided with all due

protection, particularly, in connection with concessions, incentives, in terms of guarantees, grants tax exemptions and subsidy on loans for construction of hotels even though it would certainly entail costs to the governments and other financial institutions. But it should be kept in mind that, in due course, as the industries develop and grow satisfactorily, the costs will be off-set by the gains accruing to it. Thus, the economic impact of hotel industry is the balance between the associated costs and their benefits and hence it becomes necessary for the accommodation industry to form appropriate judgements very carefully. Since hotel and tourism industries are still in their infant stages, expenditure tax on hotels should be reduced either considerably or abolished completely, at least for a specific period of time, depending upon their growth and development. In this respect, it is encouraging to note that the expenditure tax on hotels has been reduced from 20 per cent to 10 per cent as per the 1994-95 budget. However, such considerations or concessions to the resorts and other tourists destinations which are seasonal in character must prove to be still more favourable.

2. The supply of food or drinks to customers staying in a hotel does not partake the character of sale of goods. The hotel industry constitutes a distinct activity altogether to which the existing Sale of Goods Act would not apply. Imposition of sales tax on hotel services is not justifiable. Therefore sales tax on food and beverage should be abolished.
3. The rate of luxury tax varies in accordance with the volume of room sale. It also varies from state to state in India. It should be rationalized by designing an uniform structure of luxury tax throughout the nation for hotel industry. The uniform luxury tax would not create any confusion in the minds of customers. The

rate of luxury tax should be at a minimum rate as against the present rate.

4. For the development of hotel industry, hotels should enter into tie-ups with leading hotel chains in the world. These tie-ups would provide facilities for global marketing inputs, intensive training to the executives and others, consultancy services on operative systems, computer software, business meeting facilities and equipment procurement and joint participation in the international sales convention.
5. It is the duty and obligation on the part of the hoteliers to maintain a good public relation. For this purpose, a handy travel packet guide with detailed information about Indian tourism and hotel facilities and service provided. Apart from that, sales calls and seminars should be arranged frequently, inviting participants from various fields such as consultants, travel agents, employees of the hotels, government agencies and hotel association members.
6. The existing scheme of star rating and classification should be abandoned as it is a costly and unnecessary practice. Instead the new hotels should be approved by the Department of Tourism on certain quality standards as practised in other countries. The Hotel Association should evolve a self-regulatory mechanism to fulfil the objectives of quality control.
7. In South Indian hotels, the demand for rooms is higher than the supply of rooms. This situation leads to sellers' (hoteliers') market in the hotel industry. Hence, to some extent, the hoteliers are not concerned about customer satisfaction and quality of facilities and services. The Hotel Association should, therefore, form a committee which consists of hoteliers and government representatives to watch the standard of services and facilities offered by the hotels. Those hotels which are not showing co-operation in this regard, should not be given any concession or incentive and should be disapproved.

8. The boarding problems can be solved by the Tamil Nadu State Government, by framing rules and regulations for construction of more number of spacious hotels in tourist centers and taking steps for providing hygienic food and healthy environments in restaurants through government agencies like Health Department. They should also ensure that fixed prices for food items in common for all restaurants in the tourist centres, are charged.
9. The state government may also encourage the private lodge owners by relaxing the rules and regulations, for the construction of more number of hotels. The government should also fix the tariff for the various lodges taking into consideration the facilities and amenities provided.
10. It is felt that the Tamil Nadu government should take necessary steps to operate inland water transport services for passengers thorugh ferry services between Chennai and Kanyakumari connecting various tourist centers like Mamallapuram, Puduchery, Nagapattinam, Rameswaram, Thoothukudi and Tiruchendur. It will satisfy the tourists who wish to travel by sea.
11. The Tamil Nadu state government should operate more number of buses, with higher frequency to ensure "more comforts and less problems" for tourists to enable them to visit more number of tourist centers. The government of Tamil Nadu should frame rules and regulations to regulate private transport operators on war footing to protect the name and fame and increase the revenue.
12. The tourist guide problems can be solved by the Tamil Nadu State Government, by appointing sufficient number of educated, trained and approved tourist guides and purohits (Sanksrit Scholars) for the smooth understanding of the art, culture and heritage of the people of Tamil Nadu. This will help foreign tourists

and tourists from other states of India to know more about the traditional beauty of Tamil Nadu. The state government should also fix the charges for the guides in various tourist centers. Employment opportunities for the educated, unemployed youth can also be increased by this.

13. The people of Kanyakumari, especially those who are directly connected to tourism, like shop-keepers, guides, and local transport operators should be educated through "workshops" on topics like "value of tourism", "Importance of foreign exchange", "Necessity of creating name and fame of India in the foreign countries", etc. These workshops will improve not only the quality of tourism but also increase its quantity. The Central and the State governments should come forward to solve the problems involved in tourism and hotel industry. There is a need of public-private participation in solving these problems.

Conclusion

The study reveals that there is a steady increase in the arrivals of domestic as well as foreign tourists both in Tamil Nadu and Kanyakumari during the study period. Regarding the demand and supply of hotel accommodation, the highest growth rate is found among second class hotels, followed by first class and third class hotels. The selection of rooms, quality of food image of the hotel, hospitality of workers, quality of room service are found to be good. The opinion of both domestic and foreign tourists about room area and restaurant is 'good'. During peak seasons, the supply for beds is less than the demand of beds. The some important factors of hotels like health club, swimming pool facilities etc., are 'not good'. The transport facilities available also not sufficient to the tourists. The study finally concludes that Kanyakumari is a unique location and a good tourist spot in India. Therefore, the hotel owners, government, private agencies and local authorities should take necessary steps to develop Kanyakumari for promoting hotel as well as tourism industry.

Bibliography

Books

Arora, R.K. "*Heritage Tourism Management-problem and prospectives*", Mohit publications, New Delhi, 2007.

Aseem Anand, "*Advance Dictionary of Tourism*", Sarup and Sons, New Delhi, 1997.

Bhatia, A.K., "*Tourism Development Principles and Practices*", Sterling Publishers Pvt. Ltd., 2003.

Bijender Punia, K. *"Tourism Management: Problems and prospects"*, Ashish publishing House, New Delhi, 2007.

Carson Jenkins, "*Tourism in Third World Development – Fact or Fiction*", Deep and Deep Publications Private Limited, New Delhi, 2001.

Chithambara Krishna, R., "*Kaniyakumari Darsan*", Kanniyakumari Chamus Publications, 1980.

Gilham, R. *"Tourism and the media Hospitality"*, press Pvt. Ltd., Australia, 2001.

Grewal, P.S., "*Numerical Methods of Statistical Analysis*", Sterling Publishers Pvt. Ltd., New Delhi, 1987.

Laji Pathi Rai, "*Development of Tourism in India*", Printwell, Jaipur, 1993.

Maneet Kumar, "*Tourism Today - An Indian Perspective*", Kanishka Publishing House, New Delhi, 2003.

Negi, J.M.S., "*Tourism and Hoteleering: A World Wide Industry*", Gitanjali Publications, New Delhi, 1982.

Padmanabhan, S., "*In and Around Kanyakumari*", Kumar Pathippagam, Nagercoil, 2002.

Pearce and David, "*Measuring Sustainable Development*", Earthscan Publication Ltd., London, 1993.

Pran Nath Seth, "*Successful Tourism Management*", Sterling Publishers Pvt. Ltd., New Delhi, 1987.

Praveen senthil *"Hand Book of Modern Tourism"* Anmol publications, New Delhi 1999.

Ralandeep Singh, "*Dynamics of Modern Tourism*", Kanishka Publishers,

Distributors, New Delhi, 1998.

Selvam, M., "*Tourism Industry in India*", Himalaya Publishing House, Bombay, 1989.

Sudhir Andrews, "*Hotel Housekeeping Managenment and operatings*", Tata Me Graw-Hill publishing company Ltd., New Delhi, 2008.

Tha, S.M. *"Hotel Marketing"*, Himalaya publishing House, New Delhi, 2000.

Vellas Becherd Lionard, *"International Tourism"*, Macmillan press Ltd., London, 1999.

Verma, G.C., "*Tourism in Indian Context: Experiences and challenges*", Deep and Deep Publications Private Limited, New Delhi, 2004.

Journals

Oscar Braganza D. Melo and Carmelita D.Mello 'S' "Tourism in Goa Through Eco-Tourism", *Southern Economist*, Vol.46, No.18, January 15, 2008.

Abdul Malk and Aazbar "Economic and Environmental – Imapcts of tourism on socotra Island", *Southern Economist*, Vol.48, No.4, June 15, 2009.

Ajith Kumr Shukla, "Trends of Marketing management in Tourist attractions", *Indian Journal of Marketing*, Vol.xxxix, No.5, May, 2009.

Ameen A.M. Al-momani, "Tourism Development – Expectations and Apprehensions", *Monthly Commentary*, Vol.xxxvi, No.1143, June 1995.

Anbalagan, M. and Gunasekaran, "Medical Tourism in Vellore District", *Kisan world*, Vol.35, No.3, March, 2008.

Aneja and Puneet "Tourism in India – Challenges Aheead", *Kurushetra*, Vol.53, No.8, June 2005.

Anilkumar, K. "Tourism: Impact of Negative factors on the host community – case of Kerala", *The Journal of Business Studies*, Vol.4, No.8, July, 2007.

Bagri, S.C. and Suresh Bahu, A. "Impact of Terrorism of India's tourism Industry", *Southern Asian Journal of Socio-Political studies (SAJOSPS)*, Vol.10, No.1, July-December, 2009.

Bezbaruah, M.P., "Tourism – Current Scenario and Future Prospects", *Yojana*, Vol.43, No.8, August 1999.

Bheemaraj, P. "Importance of tourism in economic development: A micro study", *Southern Economist,* Vol.46, No.19, February 1, 2008.

Brij Bhardwaj, "Infrastructure for Tourism Growth", *Yojana*, Vol.43, No.8, August 1999.

Briton Stephen, "The Political Economy of Tourism in the Third World", *Annals of Tourism Research,* Vol.9, No.30, 1991.

Cees Goossens, "A Study on Tourism Information and Pleasure Motivation", *Annals of Tourism Research*, Vol. 27, No.321, 2000.

Chockalingam, S.M. and Ezhil Raji, S., "Problems and prospects of Hotel Industry" *The Journal of Business Studies*, Vol.6, No.11, January 2009.

Christina A. Joseph and Anadam P. Kavoori, "Mediated Resistance Tourism and Host Country", *Annals of Tourism Research*, Vol. 26, No.4, 2001.

Cyriac Mathew, "Diversity a Blessing to Kerala Tourism", *Southern Economist*, Vol.48, No.5, July 1, 2009.

Enrique Bigne, J. and Isabel Sanchez, M., "Tourism Image, Evaluation Variables and after Purchase Behaviour: Inter-relationship", *Tourism Management*, Vol. 22, No.5, 2001.

Francesco Frangialli, "Five Challenges for International Tourism up to the Turn of the Century", *Monthly Commentary – Blue Supplement*, Vol. xxxv, No.11, June 1994.

Garg, R.B.L., "What Ills Indian Tourism", *Southern Economist*, Vol.77, No.12, September 18, 1981.

Goichilee, "An Atractiveness of Sarawak as Ecotourism Destination: An overview of Natural – based Market Segment", *Indian Journal of Marketing*, Vol.xxxviii, No.7, July 2008.

Hall and Michael, "Ecotourism in the Australian and New Zealand Antartic Islands", *Tourism Recreation Research*, Vol. xviii, No. 2, 1993.

Harisha, N. and Jayasheela "Medical Tourism in Karnataka opportunities Galore", *Kisan world*, Vol.35, No.10, October, 2008.

Honnappa, H.C. and Ramakrishna, K.G., "Tourism development and Its impact on the Economy of Karnataka", *Southern Economist*, Vol.45, No.14, November 15, 2006.

Imanul Haque, S.M., "Dynamics of tourism Economics, India Perspective", *The Journal of Business Studies*, Vol.4, No.8, July, 2007.

Jelsy Joseph and Adalarasu, B., "A vision of Tourism sector in India", *Indian Journal of Marketing*, Vol.xxxviii, No.12, December 2008.

John, M.I., "Environmental Economics and Its Importance", *Southern Economist*, Vol.35, No. 4, June 15, 1996.

Joseph, B.K.V., "Extent of Demand for the Tourist Product of Kerala", *Southern Economist*, Vol.30, No.12, October 15, 1991.

Joseph, K.V., "Tourist Market of Kerala", *Yojana*, Vol.40, No.11, November

16-30, 1990.

Krishna, R.K. and Govindaswamy, M., "Marketing in Tourism", *Southern Economist*, Vol.36, No.22, March 15, 1998.

Kumar B. Dass and Mohanty, P.M., "Profile of Internal Tourism in India", *Southern Economist*, Vol.31, No.8, August 15, 1992.

Kuo-Ching Wang, An-Tien Hsieh, Tzung-Cheng Huan, "Critical Service Features in Group Package Tour: An Exploratory Research", *Tourism Management*, Vol.21, No. 4, 2000.

Leena Mathew and Resmi, G., "New Trends in Monsoon Tourism in Kerala", *Southern Economist*, Vol.47, No.16, December 15, 2008.

Manikanda Muthukumar, "Tourists problems in Tamilnadu", *Southern Economist*, Vol.48, No.13, November, 2009.

Manikanda Muthukumar, C., "The impact of Tourism on the socio Economic Development of Tamilnadu", *Indian Journal of Marketing*, Vol.xxxix, No.11, November, 2009.

Manjula Chaudhary, "India's image as a Tourist Destination Perspective of Foreign Tourists", *Tourism Management*, Vol.21, No.4, 2000.

Mohamed Llyas, T., "Medical Tourism: India the ight destination", *Southern Economist*, Vol.46, No.23 and 24, April 1 and 15, 2008.

Mohammad Reza Salimi sobhan, "Climate comfort from Tourism: A cas study of Anzali Township in Gilan provice Iran", *Sourthern Economist*, Vol.48, No.14, November 15, 2009.

Monisha Chattopadhyay, "Influence of Religion of Tourism: Implications for India's Tourism policy", *The Icafi Journal of consumer Behaviour*, Vol.I, No.3, 2006.

National Committee, "Tourism Industry Needs Revamp", *Southern Economist*, Vol.29, No. 2& 3, May 15 and June 1, 1990.

Nimi Dev and R., Gabriel Simon Thattil "Tourism for body and soul – 'Varkala' model", *Southern Economist*, Vol.45, No.13, August 15, 2006.

Paramasivan, G. and Sacratees, J., "Economic of tourism in Idnia", *Southern Economist*, Vol.47, No.15, December 1, 2008.

Prasain, G.P., "Touism Marketing its role in Economic development in Manipur", *SMART Journal of Business Mangement studies*, Vol.2, No.2, July – December, 2006.

Prasanta Bhattacharya, "Tourism Development", *Yojana*, Vol.48, No.12, December, 2005.

Rabindra Seth, "Tourism: Problems and Prospects", *Yojana*, Vol.43, No.8, August 1999.

Rajasenan, D. and Ajith Kumar, M.K., "Demographic, Psychographic and life style characteristies of foreign Tourists – An Expleratory study of Kerala, India", *Tourism Recreation Research*, Vol.29, No.3, 2004.

Rajitha Kumar, S., "Inter relationship between festival tourism and back water Toursism in Kerala" *The Journal of Business Studies*, Vol.5, No.9, January, 2008.

Ramesh and Olekar, "Pros and cons of Tourism Industry in India", *Kisan world*, Vol.34, No.5, May, 2007.

Renuka, R., "Role of Hospitality services in Tamil Nadu Tourism", *The IUP Journal of Management Research*, Vol.ix, No.6, October, 2010.

Revathy, S., "Tourism: India Awakens to Incredible opportunities", *Southern Economist*, Vol.46, No.20, February 15, 2008.

Ritu Galati, "Tourism in Uttaranchal – Prospects and Problems", *Yojana*, Vol.37, No.19, October 1993.

Romachandran, A. and Karthikeyan, G., "A study on tourism awareness and satisfaction in Tamil Nadu with special reference to Mamallapuram", *Indian Journal of Marketing*, Vol.xxxviii, No.11, November, 2008.

Roy, P.R., "Focus on Tourism, Blue Supplement to the Monthly Commentary of India", *Economic Conditions of Indian Institute of Public Opinion*, Vol.xxxi, No.10, May 1990.

Sankaran, A., "A study on customer perception of Tourist point in southern most corner of India", *South Asian Journal of Socio-political Studies (SAJOSPS)*, Vol.9, No.2, January – June, 2009.

Sankaran, A., "A study on customer perception on Tourist point in southern most corner of India", *South Asian Journal of Socio-political Studies (SAJOSPS)*, Vol.9, No.2, January – June, 2009.

Santhosh P. Thampi, "Ecotourism – Concept and Impacts", *Review of Social Sciences*, Vol. V, No. 1, January-June, 2004.

Sarngadharan, M., "Needs for Promotion of Tourism in India", *Employment News Weekly*, Vol.XX, No.12, New Delhi, June 17-23, 1995.

Sarngadharan, M. and Sunanda, V.S., "Effectiveness of the marketing system - A study of the ayurvedic Health Tourism", *South Asian Journal of Socio-potlitical Studies (SAJOSPS)*, Vol.10, No.1, July – December 2009.

Satyanarayana, G. and Reddiramu, M., "Sustainable Tourism: A case study of chittoor", *Southern Economist*, Vol.45, No.14, November 15, 2006.

Selvam, M., "Tourism: Social Impacts", *Kisan World*, Vol.20, No.4, April 1993.

Shivashankar Bhat, K., "Promoting Indian Tourism", *Southern Economist*, Vol.29, No.1, May 1 1990.

Shivshankar Bhat, K., "Promoting Indian Tourism", *Southern Economist*, Vol.29, No.1, May 1990.

Shrutidhar Paliwal, "Promoling Environment-Friendly Tourism", *Monthly Public Opinion Surveys*, Vol.XLII, No.4, January 1999.

Simon Wong Chak Keung, "The Study on Tourists Perceptions of Hotel Frontline Employee's Questionable Job-Related Behaviour", *Tourism Management*, Vol.21, No.10, 2000.

Singa, S.L.N., "The World Bank Atlas, World Profile People, Economy and Environment", *Southern Economist*, Vol.35, No.14, November 15, 1996.

Singh, L.P., "Tourism Marketing in India – Problems and Prospects", *Southern Economist*, Vol.29, No.18, January 1991.

Sosamma, O.P., "Tourism at Crossroads", *Commerce,* Vol.145, No.3729, November 27, 1982.

Statistical Data of WTO 1994, *Annals of Tourism Research*, Vol.23, No.3, 1996.

Subbiah, A. and Jayakumar, S., "Highway Tourism-The Indian scenario", *Kisan world*, Vol.36, No.5, May, 2009.

Sunanda, V.S., "Ayurvedie health Tourism in Kerala – wide potential for growth", *The Journal of Business Studies*, Vol.5, No.9, January, 2008.

Sunanda, V.S. and Sureshkumar, N., "Economic significance of tourism in Kerata", *Journal of Business Studies*, Vol.5, No.10, July, 2008.

Sundand, V.S., "Marketing Environment of Health Tourism in Kerala", *The Journal of Business Studies*, Vol.6, No.11, January, 2009.

Udayakumari, N., "Medical Tourism in India: An overview", *Kisan world*, Vol.34, No.5, May, 2007.

Veera Sekaran, R., "Significance of Tourism in India", *Southern Economist*, Vol.32, No.9, September 1993.

Vijaya Kumar, A., "New Strategy for Indian Tourism Industry", *Southern Economist*, Vol.37, No.11, October 1, 1998.

Vijaya Kumar, T. and Bhagavan, M.K., "Tourism the Potential", *Yojana*, Vol.37, No.15, 1992.

Yathiishkumar, "Tourism sector and sustainable Development", *Southern Economist*, Vol.46, No.9, September 1, 2007.

Yesodha Devi, N., Kanchana, V.S., "A study on customer preference and satisfaction towards restaurants in Coimbatore City", *Indian Journal of Marketing*, Vol.xxxix, No.10, October, 2009.

News Papers

Anand, N., "Arrival of Foreign Tourists: Tamil Nadu State topped Chat in 2010", *The Hindu*, February 16, 2010.

Dharmarajan, S. and Rabindra Seth, "Hotel Industry Persisting Shortage of Rooms", *The Hindu,* January 10, 1997.

Dimblebey, "Wooing the Global Hopping Tourist," *The Hindu*, February 17, 2005.

Konana and Prabhuder, "The Health Care Tourism conundrum", *The Hindu*, November 24, 2006.

Reports

Department of Tourism, Government of Tamil Nadu, Tourism Policy Note for 2001-02.

District Statistical Hand Book, Year 2002-2003, Kanyakumari.

Government of India "Tamil Nadu Development Report" Academic Foundation, New Delhi, 2007.

In and around Kanyakumari Tourist Guide Book, Published by District Collector, Kanyakumari district, Nagercoil, Co-ordination – Tourist Officer, Kanyakumari, July 2003.

Padmanabhapuram Palace – An Authentic Tourist Guide, M/s. Sree Krishna Nursing Home, Padmanabhapuram, 1997.

Tamil Nadu Tourism Development Corporation, *The Lands End*, Madras, May 1982.

Tourism Statistical Handbook 1997, Tamil Nadu and Annual Report of Tourism Department, Government of Tamil Nadu for 1998 and 1999.

Tourism Stream Action Strategy Committee of the Globe 90 Conference, "An Action Strategy for Sustainable Tourism Development", *Vancouver*, British Colombia, 1990.

World Commission on Environment and Development, *Our Common Future*, Oxford University Press, England, 1987.

Websites

Geoffrey Wall, "Ecotourism: Change Impacts and Opportunities", www.environmet_yale.edu., 2005.

George N. Wallace, "Towards a Principle Evaluation of Ecotourism Ventures", www.environment_yale.edu., 2005.

Hubb Gayman, "Five Parameters of Ecotourism", www.environment_yale.edu.., June 2003.

James Macgregor, "Developing a National Sustainable Tourism Strategy: Going Beyond Ecotourism to Protect the Planets Resources", www.ecotourism.org., 2004.

John, A.P. and Dora Pang, "Community Perceptions of Ecotourism", www.ecotourism.org., 2002.

Katrina Brandon and Richard Margolvis, "The Bothomline: Getting Biodiversity Conservation Back into Ecotourism", www.ecotourism.org., 2005.

Lori A. Gould, "Ecotourism and Sustainable Community Development", www.environment_yale.edu., 2005.

www.tamilnadu.south-india-tourism.com

www.tourism.gov.in

Index

I